ARMOR OF GOD JOURNAL

ELIZABETH R. WILLIAMS

authorHOUSE®

AuthorHouse™
1663 Liberty Drive
Bloomington, IN 47403
www.authorhouse.com
Phone: 833-262-8899

Published by AuthorHouse 09/27/2023

ISBN: 979-8-8230-1189-1 (sc)
ISBN: 979-8-8230-1188-4 (e)

Beautiful people

This Journal Belongs To:

_____

Belt of Truth

Ephesians 6:14

To wear this belt, we must live a truth-based life. A dishonest Christian is helpless in the face of the adversary. Allowing the Holy Spirit to guide us guarantees that we are not driven by the flesh when we live in line with the Holy Spirit. The enemy will try to damage us through our weaknesses, the environment, and ancestral curses. When you live by God's truth, you realize you are no longer a part of the world, and that God has greater expectations for you. Jesus demonstrated God's truth to you and wants you to express and embrace it. No matter what, Jesus always told the truth in love and was unafraid to defend the weak. Jesus didn't give any thought to a person's position since he knew GOD was over everyone else position or authority.

Breastplate of Righteousness

Ephesians 6:14

Living a moral life is treating people better than you would like to be treated in return. We are maintaining innocence in front of the Lord. Living a holy life is your righteousness. Not just saying it; doing it. Be sincere, modest, and kind. On the other hand, the adversary is also on a mission to undermine the works God has given us through whatever openings related to our lives so that we may put it this way: everyone is on God's assignment.

REFLECTION

_____

_____

_____

_____

_____

_____

_____

_____

_____

_____

_____

_____

_____

_____

_____

Gospel of Peace

Ephesians 6:15

Possess a solid knowledge and comprehension of the Gospel. Tell everyone about the good news of Jesus Christ. The adversary is cunning; he knows that we value the people in our lives, which is why, most of the time, he manipulates those individuals to cause our misery and melancholy, make us feel hopeless and heartbroken, and prevent us from trusting those close to us. The example of Jesus and the disciples teaches us that we will face opposition even while spreading the gospel. However, even in the face of adversity, put confidence in God to give you lasting peace that no one or anything can take away.

Shield of Faith

Ephesians 6:16

Protect yourself with faith from the flaming darts the adversary throws at you. Escape sin. Your faith protects you from the enemy's falsehoods and enables you to cling to God's promises. Because we are His children, God utilizes the circumstances the adversary has placed in our lives to reroute us when He wants to save us. Even if it may appear that everything is going according to plan or that everything is crumbling, His glory still rules in these situations. While it may appear like the adversary is at work, God first strengthens your defenses by establishing boundaries.

REFLECTION

_____

_____

_____

_____

_____

_____

_____

_____

_____

_____

_____

_____

_____

_____

Helmet of Salvation

Ephesians 6:17

Have faith that Jesus died to atone for your sins. No matter what the world says about our Savior, believe in Jesus. Walk with assurance while anticipating His return. When putting on your helmet of salvation, your mind must be renewed. Your mind must be trained to conquer the challenges you will encounter in life. The Bible should always be our foundation. God knows and understands us best, and He knows that's the only way He could create limits for us, much like gold goes through fire to make it pure, so He can arrive at a precise moment when we're suffering, not to decrease or erase the pain. We endure suffering to grow stronger and more conscious of God's rescuing power.

Sword of the Spirit

Ephesians 6:17

The Word of God defends us. People receive truth, love, and hope from the Bible. The Bible is our offensive tool. Use it to express the Truth to others around you lovingly. Combat with God's Word in mind. These are techniques for erecting a wall of defense to keep the adversary at bay and through reading the word, sharing the word, living by the word. fasting, repenting, praying, and submitting our families and lives to God. We are firmly rooted in God's word and confident that everything we say reflects God's truth.

REFLECTION

_____

_____

_____

_____

_____

_____

_____

_____

_____

_____

_____

_____

_____

_____

From Ephesians 6:14-16 (NIV)

The 7 Pieces of the Armor of GOD are:

1. Belt of Truth

2. Breastplate of Righteousness

3. Feet fitted with the Gospel of Peace

4. Shield of Faith

5. Helmet of Salvation

6. Sword of the Spirit – The Word of God

7. A lifestyle of praying without ceasing

Ephesians 6:21, Colossians 4:7-9, and Philemon 1:10–12 all state that Paul wrote the epistle to the Ephesians somewhere between AD 60 and 61. Paul also wrote Colossians and Philemon at the same time. Paul was serving his first Roman jail sentence (Ephesians 3:1; 4:1), making Ephesians one of the four letters that have come to be known as the jail Epistles. Our Armor is divine protection, right standing with God, conforming to the ways of God, and falling in love with God.

Christians today are able to identify the many pieces of armor that we put on and how they serve to shield us from harm and support us in battle. The belt, breastplate, sandals (shoes), shield, helmet, and sword are all parts of the celestial armor. The only piece of God's armor that may be used offensively is the sword; the other pieces are entirely defensive. We may battle false doctrine and subdue evil by relying on God's word.

I am THE WAY the TRUTH, and the Life. No one comes to the FATHER except through ME.

John 14:6

be STRONG AND courageous DO NOT BE AFRAID do not be DISCOURAGED FOR THE LORD your GOD will be WITH you WHEREVER you GO →

JOSHUA 1:9

ELIZABETH R. WILLIAMS

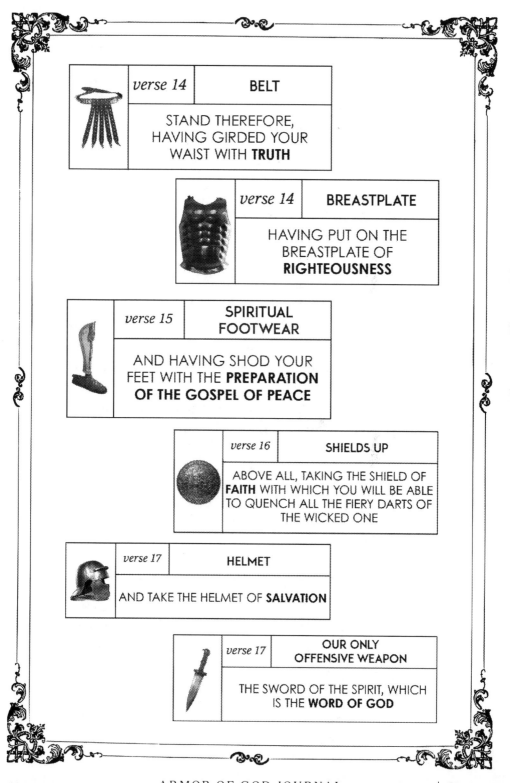

	verse 14	**BELT**
	STAND THEREFORE, HAVING GIRDED YOUR WAIST WITH **TRUTH**	

	verse 14	**BREASTPLATE**
	HAVING PUT ON THE BREASTPLATE OF **RIGHTEOUSNESS**	

	verse 15	**SPIRITUAL FOOTWEAR**
	AND HAVING SHOD YOUR FEET WITH THE **PREPARATION OF THE GOSPEL OF PEACE**	

	verse 16	**SHIELDS UP**
	ABOVE ALL, TAKING THE SHIELD OF **FAITH** WITH WHICH YOU WILL BE ABLE TO QUENCH ALL THE FIERY DARTS OF THE WICKED ONE	

	verse 17	**HELMET**
	AND TAKE THE HELMET OF **SALVATION**	

	verse 17	**OUR ONLY OFFENSIVE WEAPON**
	THE SWORD OF THE SPIRIT, WHICH IS THE **WORD OF GOD**	

"Armor" refers to both offensive weapons and defense mechanisms that shield the soldier from injury. The phrase "armor of God" makes me think of two verses from the book of Isaiah. The first, recorded in Isaiah 11:1–10, shows the Messiah as being covered with the righteousness and faithfulness of God, moving about to rescue God's oppressed people (see Isa. 10:24–34), slaying the wicked, gathering Israel, attracting the Gentiles, and establishing God's dominion in a universe that has just been created.

Jesus is shown as having the power to destroy the wicked in Isaiah 11:4-5. He also describes how his righteousness will envelop him. God's servant is heard saying in Isa 49:2: "He sharpened the edge of my mouth." The feet of the messenger of good news are mentioned in Isaiah 52:7. God is supposed to wear righteousness as a breastplate and a helmet of salvation on his head in Isaiah 59:17. When Paul talks about a Christian putting on the whole armor of God, bowing under the weight of the truth is the first thing he brings up.

The texts in the Bible were written by the apostles under the guidance of the Holy Spirit. So that we would have something to use as a guide for living, so that we would learn more about life and the best way to live it, these scriptures were written by the Apostles with the help of the Holy Spirit. All of the Bible is said to be inspired by God, trustworthy for revealing divine truths, and effective for rebuking, correcting, and instructing in righteousness, according to 2 Timothy 3:16. This indicates that the Holy Spirit's inspiration was used to produce the whole Bible.

REFLECTION

_____

_____

_____

_____

_____

_____

_____

_____

_____

_____

_____

_____

_____

_____

Ephesians 6:10-18(NIV)

Finally, be strong in the Lord and in his mighty power. Put on the whole armor of God, so that you can take your stand against the devil's schemes. For our struggle is not against flesh and blood, but against the rulers, against the authorities, against the powers of this dark world, and against spiritual forces of evil in the heavenly realms. Therefore put on the full armor of God, so that when the day of evil comes, you may be able to stand your ground, and after you have done everything, to stand. Stand firm then, with the belt of truth buckled around your waist, with the breastplate of righteousness in place, and with your feet fitted with the readiness that comes from the gospel of peace. In addition to all of this, take up the shield of faith, with which, you can extinguish all the flaming arrows of the evil one. Take the helmet of salvation, and the sword of the Spirit, which is the word of God; And pray in the Spirit on all occasions with all kinds of prayers and requests. With this in mind, be alert and always keep on praying for all the Lord's people.

ELIZABETH R. WILLIAMS

"pray without ceasing"
1 Thessalonians 5:17 (KJV)

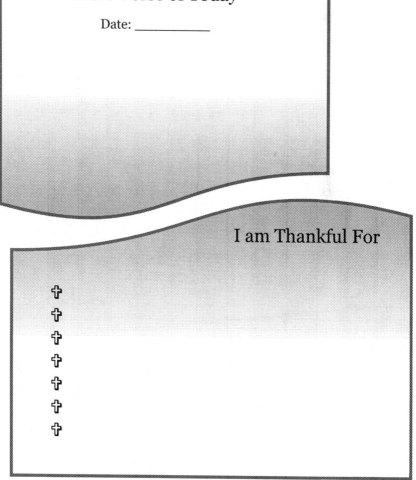

Bible Verse of Today

Date: _____

I am Thankful For

✝
✝
✝
✝
✝
✝
✝

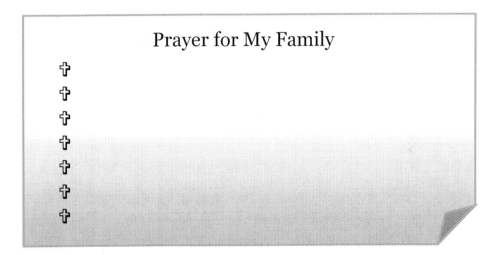

Prayer for My Family

✝
✝
✝
✝
✝
✝
✝

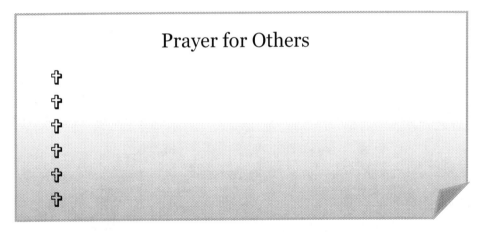

Prayer for Others

✝
✝
✝
✝
✝
✝

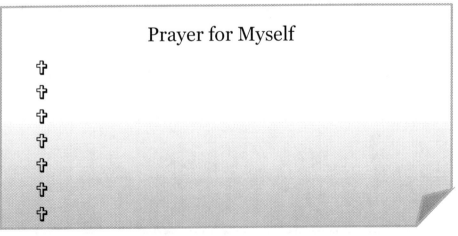

Prayer for Myself

✝
✝
✝
✝
✝
✝
✝

ELIZABETH R. WILLIAMS

REFLECTION

_____

_____

_____

_____

_____

_____

_____

_____

_____

_____

_____

WORD SEARCH

```
W  C  H  H  R  L  T  O  R  Y  I  E  U  B  G
T  Y  E  G  I  C  S  O  A  P  V  E  N  N  B
S  W  L  U  O  B  I  A  R  A  Z  N  O  Y  E
E  Y  M  M  V  R  W  J  R  O  B  R  I  G  Z
Z  F  E  E  R  R  T  B  A  D  T  I  H  X  K
A  N  T  A  J  E  S  U  S  S  K  C  B  Z  R
C  E  W  O  S  T  A  N  D  F  I  R  M  L  N
C  V  L  S  M  P  A  U  L  A  E  Z  U  B  E
W  X  C  W  R  H  G  P  G  E  N  E  R  A  L
Y  R  O  O  P  J  N  A  Q  O  K  W  H  D  V
R  J  U  R  R  P  R  O  T  E  C  T  I  O  N
G  H  R  D  A  Z  T  A  E  L  X  U  S  V  W
C  W  A  B  Y  W  O  R  D  O  F  G  O  D  Y
O  I  G  K  E  S  I  X  D  B  L  Q  P  X  F
L  N  E  C  R  E  B  A  Z  O  W  X  R  K  I
```

JESUS	WARRIOR	STRONG
SIX	PRAYER	PROTECTION
BIBLE	HELMET	STAND FIRM
SWORD	GENERAL	BRAVE
PAUL	WORD OF GOD	COURAGE

ELIZABETH R. WILLIAMS

Use the letters below to describe yourself or your victory

S _____

T _____

R _____

E _____

N _____

G _____

T _____

H _____

"For if, by the trespass of the one man, death reigned through that one man, how much more will those who receive God's abundant provision of grace and of the gift of righteousness reign in life through the one man, Jesus Christ!" Romans 5:17 (NIV)

ELIZABETH R. WILLIAMS

The armor of the believers is likewise kept together by the truth. The human person of Jesus Christ and the written Word of God both contains the Ultimate Truth. (John 14:6) If we want to safeguard ourselves from our bodies, the outside world, and the Father of Lies, we must be aware of this Truth. It serves to remind us of who we are in Christ and provides us with a feeling of purpose.

A breastplate was frequently carried by Roman soldiers. When he was too slow to get his shield back during combat, this armor shielded his essential organs. The breastplate protected the wearer from the enemy's swift, rapid advances.

Romans 3:23-26 (NIV) for all have sinned and fall short of the glory of God, and all are justified freely by his grace through the redemption that came by Christ Jesus. God presented Christ as a sacrifice of atonement,[a] through the shedding of his blood—to be received by faith. He did this to demonstrate his righteousness because in his forbearance he had left the sins committed beforehand unpunished— he did it to demonstrate his righteousness at the present time, so as to be just and the one who justifies those who have faith in Jesus.

Roman troops used sandals (shoes) to protect their feet. The purpose of these shoes was to preserve troops' feet during their arduous marches into battle. They have extremely thick soles that were perfectly fitted around their ankles to prevent blisters. Caligae also had spikes on the bottom, which improved mobility. They were given a strong foundation because of this. The Gospel also gives Christians a strong foundation. We have peace because of what Jesus has done for us as followers of Christ.

REFLECTION

_____

_____

_____

_____

_____

_____

_____

_____

_____

_____

_____

_____

_____

_____

Roman warriors had advanced armor, including shields. The scutum, or shield, was a soldier's first line of defense. To put out the enemy's blazing arrows, it could be plunged in the water. It was made of indestructible wood, leather, canvas, and metal.

Faith is the believer's defense. Faith in God's omnipotence and security is necessary to maintain stability. According to Romans 8:28, those who love God and have been called in accordance with his purpose are blessed in all that he does. Never should we forget that God arranges things for our ultimate good. He always honors His promises.

The believer's helmet of salvation is the most crucial component of a Christian's defense. Without the Holy Spirit's indwelling, which a believer receives at the time of salvation, every other armor is ineffectual. Christians have the power to fight because of salvation. In times of weakness, it protects us. If there is no salvation, there is no victory.

The brain of the soldier is one of the most exposed areas. Without his helmet, one blow to the head would be fatal. His helmet covered his entire head, except the area between his eyes. His armor wouldn't do him any good if he didn't have his helmet.

The soldier's sword is not a defensive weapon, in contrast to all his other equipment. The sword was a weapon that may be dangerous. In the hands of a skilled warrior, he was capable of piercing even the strongest armor. According to Hebrews 4:12-13, the Bible is alive and active, sharper than any two-edged weapon, penetrating to the dividing of the soul and spirit, of joints and marrow, and discerning the thoughts and intentions of the heart. Our tool is the written and active Word of God. Every extra line of protection protects us against attacks. The tools we need to fight and defeat all enemies are provided for us in God's Word. Christ used the Bible to combat the devil as he was being tempted in the desert.

Matthew 4:8-11 (NIV) Again, the devil took him to a very high mountain and showed him all the kingdoms of the world and their splendor. "All this I will give you," he said, "if you will bow down and worship me." Jesus said to him, "Away from me, Satan! It is written: 'Worship the Lord your God and serve him only. Then the devil left him, and angels came and attended him.

The written and active Word of God is our weapon. Every additional layer of defense shields us from assaults. In God's Word, we find the weapons we need to confront and vanquish all foes. The sword of the Spirit is the fundamental tool God has given us to wield against the devil, the influences of the world, and our sinful nature.

REFLECTION

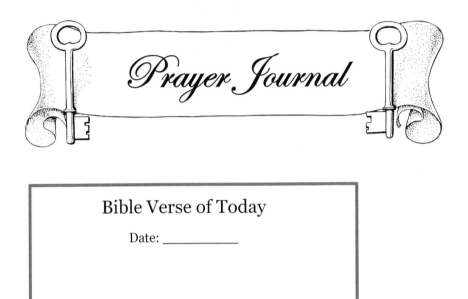

Bible Verse of Today

Date: _____

I am Thankful For

✝

✝

✝

✝

✝

✝

✝

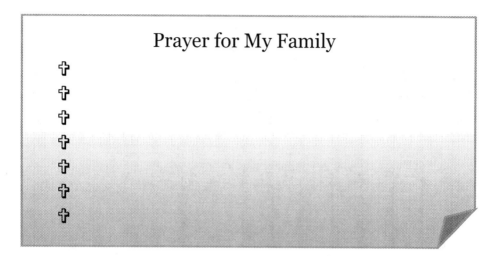

Prayer for My Family

✝
✝
✝
✝
✝
✝
✝

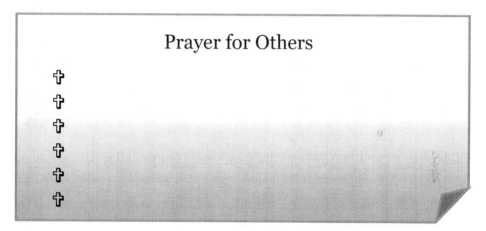

Prayer for Others

✝
✝
✝
✝
✝
✝

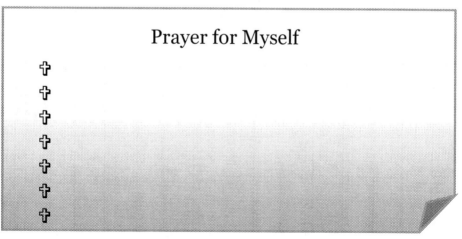

Prayer for Myself

✝
✝
✝
✝
✝
✝
✝

REFLECTION

_____

_____

_____

_____

_____

_____

_____

_____

_____

_____

_____

_____

WORD SEARCH

```
G N T B E A R T H U E D L O T
U S N F N I G H T X L Q I R R
B Y E L Y D R H K C Z X G P E
R Z V A G Y C E O I H D H T E
W J D G M U N A Y A N T T L S
O W Y N R A E V J A A M F L V
P C I T F X N E L P M U R O H
E L E S G K R N D V Q O P M A
F Z A A A V O S K J X G O W C
I W X N N Y N S M H U E Z N B
J A D S T S Q K P C N E M N L
F A S N U S R Y T U L V A J O
D Z N I T W U C S J Q M R K X
Q H W A T E R S J R O N G Z C
Q X B D N V A T U W E Z L J F
```

HEAVENS	MAN	PLANTS
SKY	WATERS	TREES
MOON	OCEANS	DAY
EARTH	WOMAN	SUN
LAND	LIGHT	

Use the letters below to describe
yourself or your victory

A _____

R _____

M _____

O _____

R _____

O _____

F _____

G _____

O _____

D _____

ELIZABETH R. WILLIAMS

"Now faith is confidence in what we hope for and assurance about what we do not see."
Hebrews 11:1 (NIV)

_____

_____

_____

_____

_____

_____

_____

_____

_____

_____

_____

_____

_____

_____

Spiritual battles occur every day in our world. We all engage in a spiritual conflict with a real adversary. "The thief only comes to steal, murder, and destroy; I have come that they may have life, and enjoy it to the full.", (John 10:10, NIV) Our enemy's primary goals are to steal, murder, and destroy. Hence, all he desires is to bring about defeat. However, our enemy is also aware of the fact that we belong to God. We have inherited the mark of Jesus Christ.

Our lives are part of God's design. God has a plan for each of our lives, and we must also understand that the opposition has a strategic plan of attack for our lives as well. All we have to do is to choose who we will listen to and whose voice we will follow each day. We must decide to put on the full armor of God each day. If we make a firm commitment to follow Jesus each day, we will ultimately avoid falling into the devil's snare.

"The thief comes only to steal and kill and destroy; I have come that they may have life and have it to the full." John 10:10 (NIV)

Beautiful friend, Let's pray:

Repeat after me: Angels of God extinguish every demonic gathering working against my life, family, business, education, ministry, and career. I decree that the Lord has seen my pain and will never remain silent. In the mighty name of Jesus, the Lord will come to my assistance immediately.

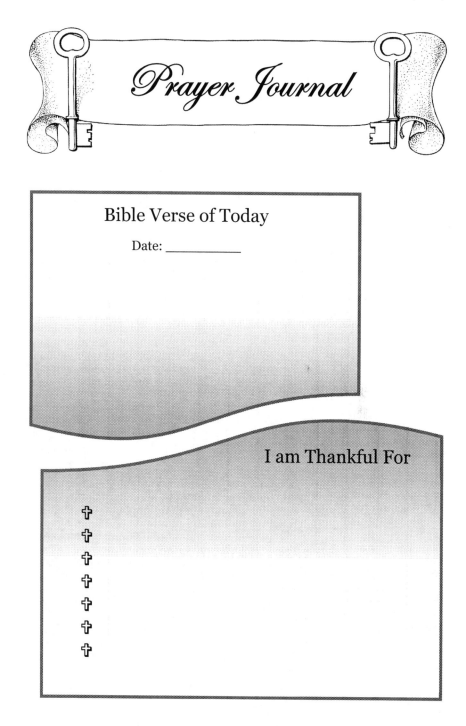

Prayer Journal

Bible Verse of Today

Date: _____

I am Thankful For

✝

✝

✝

✝

✝

✝

✝

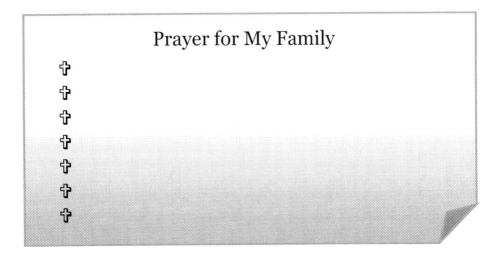

Prayer for My Family

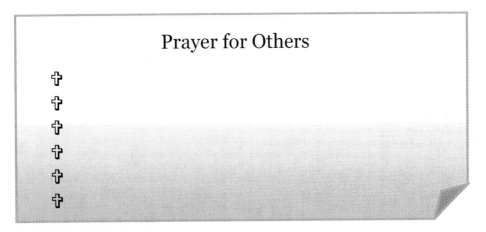

Prayer for Others

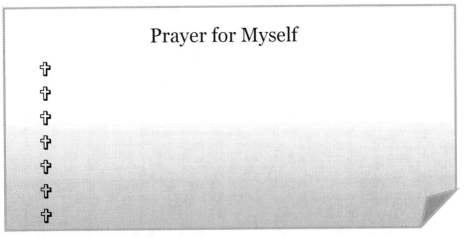

Prayer for Myself

ELIZABETH R. WILLIAMS

REFLECTION

_____

_____

_____

_____

_____

_____

_____

_____

_____

_____

_____

_____

_____

WORD SEARCH

```
R  I  R  V  E  P  H  E  S  I  A  N  S  K  G
X  U  G  I  S  B  P  I  D  E  L  O  H  I  M
B  O  A  L  G  T  G  S  S  H  I  E  L  D  X
Z  R  N  Y  E  H  I  H  S  B  F  T  G  O  X
Z  J  E  M  O  I  T  Q  N  B  U  K  M  S  T
U  S  L  A  T  K  F  E  S  W  O  R  D  J  D
S  E  T  F  S  R  O  H  O  P  A  U  L  O  X
H  A  S  R  A  T  U  F  Z  U  Q  D  G  U  C
W  R  L  E  E  I  P  T  A  H  S  F  N  K  G
J  I  P  V  Q  N  T  L  H  R  O  N  G  L  T
S  F  E  Z  A  P  G  H  A  D  R  X  E  M  V
E  B  A  B  I  T  T  T  R  T  N  O  Z  S  S
P  R  C  K  E  A  I  O  H  O  E  Y  W  L  S
Q  B  E  I  V  L  W  O  F  E  E  T  Z  S  S
G  Q  X  Y  H  A  T  W  N  P  R  A  Y  E  R
```

FAITH
FEET
EPHESIANS
RIGHTEOUSNESS
ARROWS
TRUTH

SWORD
PAUL
PRAYER
SALVATION
HELMET
PEACE

ELOHIM
STRENGTH
BREASTPLATE
SHIELD
BELT

ELIZABETH R. WILLIAMS

Use the letters below to describe yourself or your victory

P
_____

R
_____

A
_____

Y
_____

E
_____

R
_____

"If anyone destroys God's temple, God will destroy that person; for God's temple is sacred, and you together are that temple." 1 Corinthians 3:17 *(NIV)*

_____

_____

_____

_____

_____

_____

_____

_____

_____

_____

_____

_____

_____

_____

_____

ELIZABETH R. WILLIAMS

Beautiful friend, Let's pray:

According to Psalm 55:22 (NIV), when I give my worries to the Lord, He sustains me and never allows the righteous to be shaken. As in the time of Midian, Lord, break the oppressor's rod and the enemy's yoke (Isaiah 9:4, NIV). In the name of Jesus, may every burden of disease, want, and servitude be broken. (NIV, Galatians 5:1). In the name of Jesus, may every burden be removed from my life (Zechariah 12:3, NIV). I embrace the liberation from which Jesus has released in my life. The weight I carry is light because of Jesus (Matthew 11:30, NIV).

"pray without ceasing"
1 Thessalonians 5:17 (KJV)

Prayer Journal

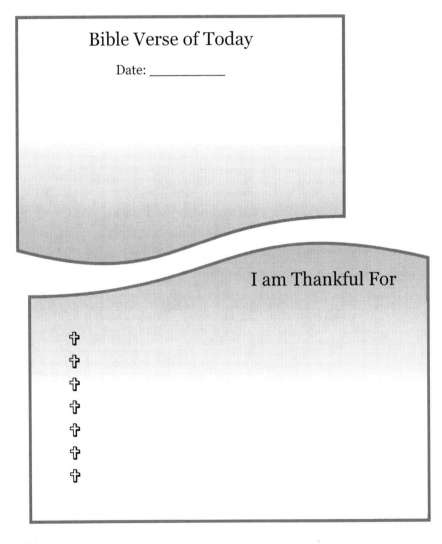

Bible Verse of Today

Date: _____

I am Thankful For

✝

✝

✝

✝

✝

✝

✝

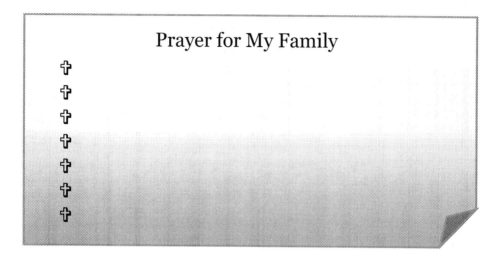

Prayer for My Family

✟

✟

✟

✟

✟

✟

✟

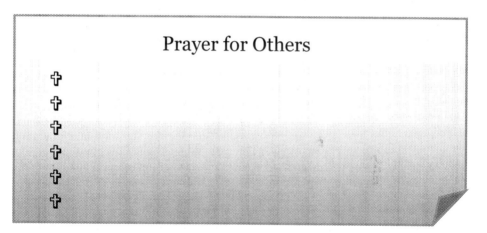

Prayer for Others

✟

✟

✟

✟

✟

✟

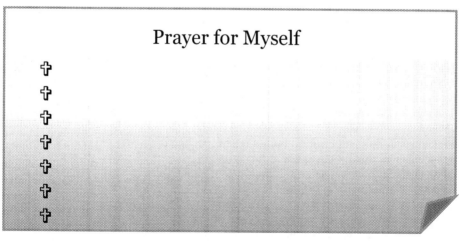

Prayer for Myself

✟

✟

✟

✟

✟

✟

✟

REFLECTION

_____

_____

_____

_____

_____

_____

_____

_____

_____

_____

_____

_____

WORD SEARCH

```
E H A S U T B J N N E L X J E
Z P F L P H L L U U V E B I X
J N H P A L Q E M D M Z S R O
E Z G E U M N O V B G B G Q D
R N E S S K E V I I F E E E U
E C N A D I E N R S T Z S R S
M Y E M I S A K T L A I F A S
I L S U U H T N V A O I C A M
A J I E Q A K E S W T C A U P
H M S L H P U A N J F I Z H S
E C C L E S I A S T E S O U E
Y E H W F R J C P B S M K N O
B Z X T R O G Z M C U L F D S
S R D E U T E R O N O M Y C Y
U A O B A D I A H J O S H U A
```

GENESIS   **OBADIAH**   **CHRONICLES**
EXODUS   **LAMENTATIONS**   **EZRA**
LEVITICUS   **ECCLESIASTES**   **ISAIAH**
NUMBERS   **DEUTERONOMY**   **JUDGES**
JOSHUA   **SAMUEL**   **JEREMIAH**

Use the letters below to describe
yourself or your victory

P _____

R _____

O _____

T _____

E _____

C _____

T _____

I _____

O _____

N _____

ELIZABETH R. WILLIAMS

"Come to me, all you who are weary and burdened, and I will give you rest. Take my yoke upon you and learn from me, for I am gentle and humble in heart, and you will find rest for your souls. For my yoke is easy and my burden is light."
Matthew 11:28-30 (NIV)

Beautiful friend, Let's pray:

Holy Spirit, we put on all of our armor pieces today, to protect our lives. We put on the belt of truth to shield ourselves against deceit and falsehoods. To guard against the temptations we face, we put on the breastplate of righteousness. We have the message of peace in our hearts today, and we are ready to spread your light wherever you lead us. Instead of letting worry and fear control our lives, we choose to live in the freedom and peace of your Holy Spirit. We embrace your shield of faith, which will protect us from whatever arrows and threats the adversary may direct at us. We believe in your power to protect us and choose to trust in you.

Jesus, we put our confidence in you because we know you have the ability to keep us safe. We put on the helmet of salvation, which protects our minds and thoughts and serves as a reminder that, according to Ephesians 1:5, God has predestined us to be adopted as sons through Jesus Christ, in accordance with his pleasure and will, and rescued by the grace of Christ Jesus. The only offensive tool you have given us for battle—the sword of the Spirit—is sharper than any two-edged sword and has the ability to overthrow strongholds. It is your very Word. We are victorious always.

Thank you Jesus, that you continually work for us, shielding, protecting, strengthening, exposing acts of evil, bringing to light what needs to be known, and covering us from the violent attacks we experience even while we are unaware. In the magnificent name of Jesus, Amen.

Prayer Journal

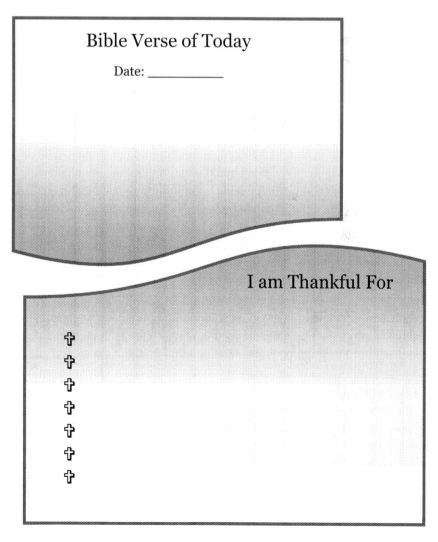

Bible Verse of Today

Date: _____

I am Thankful For

✝
✝
✝
✝
✝
✝
✝

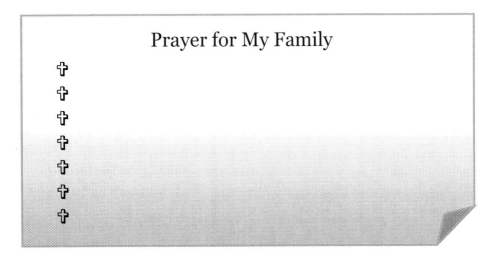

Prayer for My Family

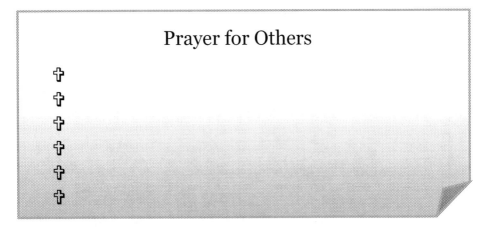

Prayer for Others

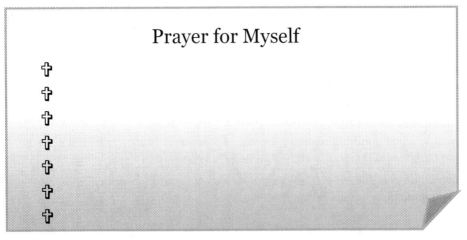

Prayer for Myself

ELIZABETH R. WILLIAMS

REFLECTION

_____

_____

_____

_____

_____

_____

_____

_____

_____

_____

_____

_____

_____

_____

WORD SCRABBLE

1) e i a p s n h s e   _____

2) y r a p e r   _____

3) o r a r r i w   _____

4) s x i   _____

5) e s j s u   _____

6) a p u l   _____

7) o c u e g r a   _____

8) d s r e o i l   _____

9) n d i a f m s r t   _____

10) r h s n t g e t   _____

11) h e i l o m   _____

12) e v a r b   _____

13) o g r o f d o d w   _____

14) e i b b l   _____

15) l e e g n a r   _____

Use the letters below to describe
yourself or your victory

C _____

O _____

U _____

R _____

A _____

G _____

E _____

"I will repay you for the years the locusts have eaten the great locust and the young locust, the other locusts, and the locust swarm my great army that I sent among you. You will have plenty to eat until you are full, and you will praise the name of the Lord your God, who has worked wonders for you; never again will my people be shamed." Joel 2:25-26 (NIV)

Beautiful friend, Let's pray:
Holy Spirit, equip me today with the armor of God.

I put on the belt of truth (Verse 14). May Your truth rule in my thoughts, emotions, and voice today.

I put the breastplate of righteousness (Verse 14).

Without You, Jesus, there is no righteousness. I have been "redeemed" through Jesus and made righteous in Your sight. Help me to lead an upright life.

When I put on the shoes of peace, I pray that they will be solidly grounded on the good news of what Jesus achieved on the cross (verse 15).

So that I might shine Jesus' light and encourage others to seek You out, Lord, mercifully give me the ability to reflect the gospel in both my words and my actions.

To protect myself from any blazing arrows that may be directed at me, I put on the armor of faith (verse 16). We are appreciative of our triumph in Christ. God has everything under control, no matter what the enemy may use to attack us.

I wore the helmet of my salvation (verse 17).

Lord, guard my thoughts and constantly reassure me that nothing can ever divert my attention from You. By grace and trust, I have found salvation.

I grasp the sword of the Spirit, the Word of God (verse 17).

As I study Your Word, Lord, may Your Holy Spirit broaden my intellect and heart and enable me to discover new things about You. Please help me to be ready and "filled by the Holy Spirit" I need your help to learn Your Word and to memorize it. God provides me with daily strength. Lord, please always remind me to pray in the Spirit (verse 18). Help me to be steadfast in my prayer life with you. Holy Spirit urges me to remain aware, content, and grateful always. In the wonderful name of Jesus.

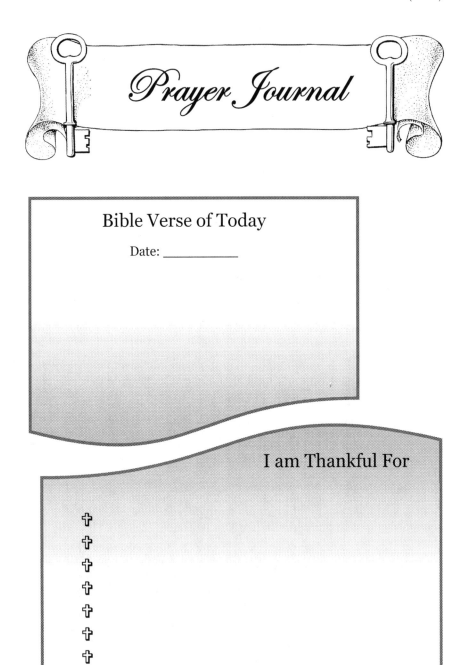

Bible Verse of Today

Date: _____

I am Thankful For

✝

✝

✝

✝

✝

✝

✝

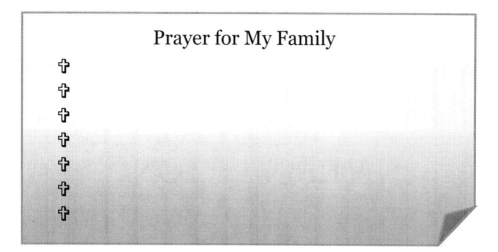

Prayer for My Family

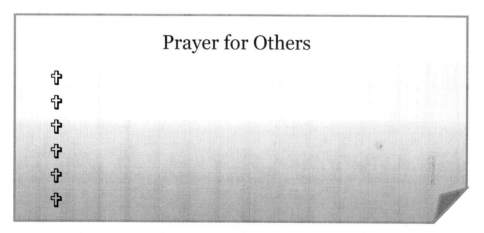

Prayer for Others

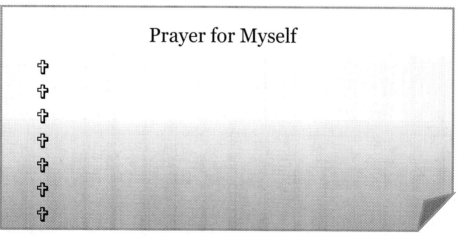

Prayer for Myself

REFLECTION

_____

_____

_____

_____

_____

_____

_____

_____

_____

_____

_____

_____

_____

_____

WORD SEARCH

```
O  R  G  K  I  Y  Y  M  U  B  A  Q  S  C  N
Z  F  U  M  O  S  G  T  A  G  A  I  N  S  T
U  Q  A  J  Y  F  E  V  J  T  E  L  D  L  W
P  F  Q  I  L  Z  N  D  A  H  C  O  R  K  J
W  E  V  E  T  N  T  D  F  G  C  N  U  Z  T
M  G  A  U  O  H  L  Q  V  K  Z  G  D  S  M
X  E  I  C  Q  E  E  Y  G  J  C  S  K  N  P
V  N  E  R  E  I  N  O  W  Y  A  U  J  K  M
F  P  R  K  H  L  E  E  T  J  A  F  S  M  Z
U  R  W  E  N  T  S  Q  R  E  C  F  L  B  H
Z  Y  U  U  K  E  S  L  V  H  M  E  X  C  V
X  F  S  I  J  P  S  O  H  N  D  R  K  C  Q
I  P  Q  H  T  K  L  S  B  D  V  I  L  T  J
T  E  M  P  E  R  A  N  C  E  A  N  S  U  V
H  O  L  Y  S  P  I  R  I  T  W  G  L  A  W
```

HOLY SPIRIT	FAITH	TEMPERANCE
LOVE	LONG	MEEKNESS
JOY	SUFFERING	FRUIT
AGAINST	LAW	
PEACE	GENTLENESS	

Use the letters below to describe yourself or your victory

H _____

O _____

P _____

E _____

ELIZABETH R. WILLIAMS

> *"For the Lord your God moves about in your camp to protect you and to deliver your enemies to you. Your camp must be holy, so that he will not see among you anything indecent and turn away from you." Deuteronomy 23:14 (NIV)*

Bible Verse of Today

Date: _____

I am Thankful For

✝
✝
✝
✝
✝
✝
✝

ELIZABETH R. WILLIAMS

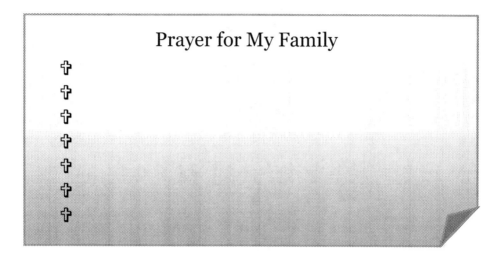

Prayer for My Family

✝

✝

✝

✝

✝

✝

✝

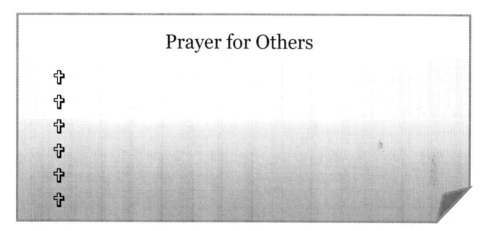

Prayer for Others

✝

✝

✝

✝

✝

✝

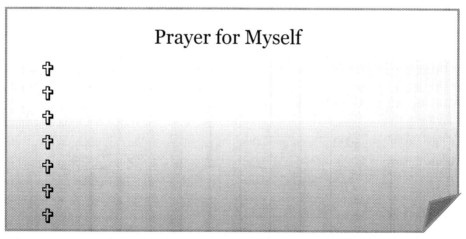

Prayer for Myself

✝

✝

✝

✝

✝

✝

✝

REFLECTION

_____

_____

_____

_____

_____

_____

_____

_____

_____

_____

_____

_____

_____

_____

Use the letters below to describe
yourself or your victory

F _____

A _____

I _____

T _____

H _____

"But let all who take refuge in you be glad; let them ever sing for joy. Spread your protection over them, that those who love your name may rejoice in you."
Psalm 5:11 (NIV)

_____

_____

_____

_____

_____

_____

_____

_____

_____

_____

_____

_____

_____

_____

_____

_____

ELIZABETH R. WILLIAMS

"pray without ceasing"
1 Thessalonians 5:17 (KJV)

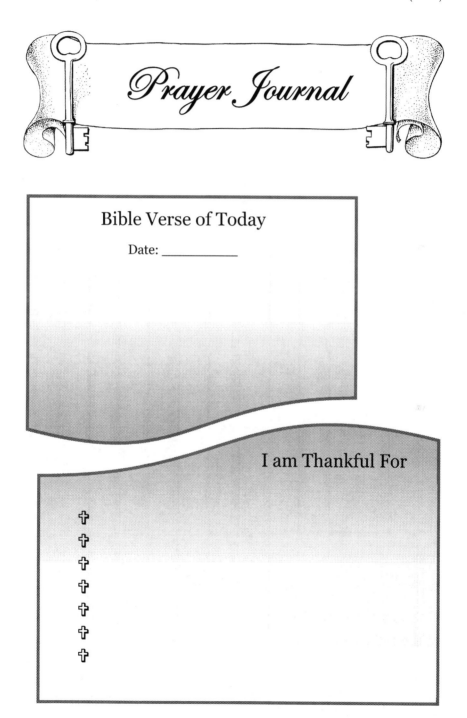

Bible Verse of Today

Date: _____

I am Thankful For

✝
✝
✝
✝
✝
✝
✝

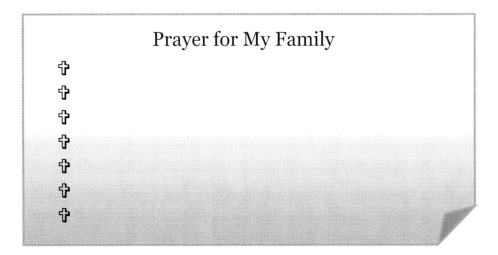

Prayer for My Family

✟
✟
✟
✟
✟
✟
✟

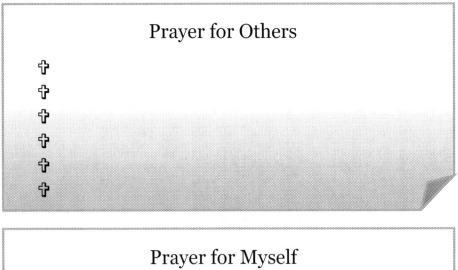

Prayer for Others

✟
✟
✟
✟
✟
✟

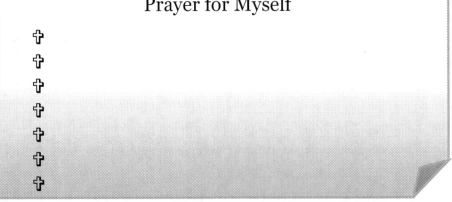

Prayer for Myself

✟
✟
✟
✟
✟
✟
✟

REFLECTION

_____

_____

_____

_____

_____

_____

_____

_____

_____

_____

_____

_____

_____

Use the letters below to describe yourself or your victory

J

U

S

T

I

C

E

ELIZABETH R. WILLIAMS

Beautiful friend, Let's pray:

In the great name of Jesus Christ, I announce and pronounce that the strongholds of procrastination and delay are being demolished. You won't have to go through unfavorable circumstances anymore. I decree you are moving in a measure of victory. In the name of Jesus, I pray that angels will be sent to help you achieve your goals.

"You, Lord, will keep the needy safe and will protect us forever from the wicked." Psalm 12:7 *(NIV)*

_____

_____

_____

_____

_____

_____

_____

_____

_____

_____

_____

_____

_____

_____

_____

ELIZABETH R. WILLIAMS

"pray without ceasing"
1 Thessalonians 5:17 (KJV)

Prayer Journal

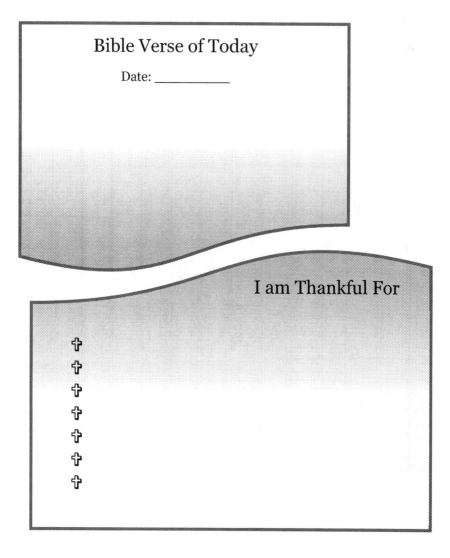

Bible Verse of Today

Date: _____

I am Thankful For

✝

✝

✝

✝

✝

✝

✝

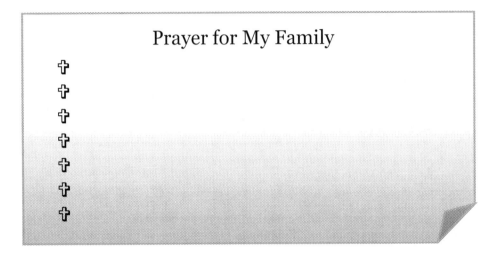

Prayer for My Family

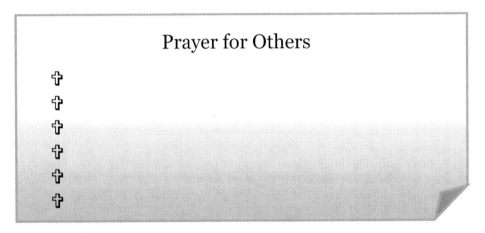

Prayer for Others

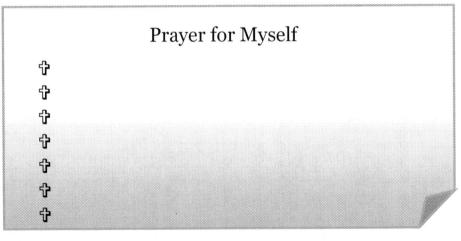

Prayer for Myself

ELIZABETH R. WILLIAMS

REFLECTION

_____

_____

_____

_____

_____

_____

_____

_____

_____

_____

_____

_____

Use the letters below to describe
yourself or your victory

T

_____

R

_____

U

_____

T

_____

H

_____

ELIZABETH R. WILLIAMS

"May integrity and uprightness protect me, because my hope, Lord, is in you." Psalm 25:21 (NIV)

_____

_____

_____

_____

_____

_____

_____

_____

_____

_____

_____

_____

_____

_____

Prayer Journal

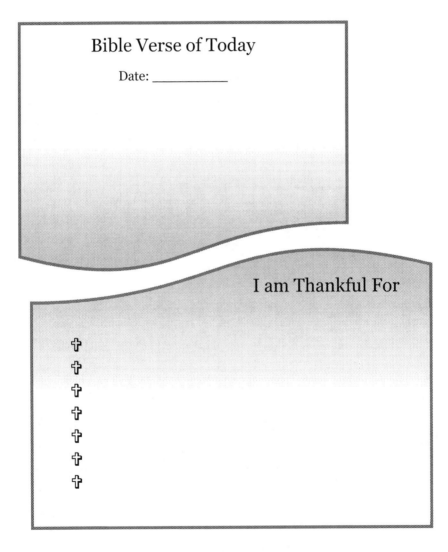

Bible Verse of Today

Date: _____

I am Thankful For

✝
✝
✝
✝
✝
✝
✝

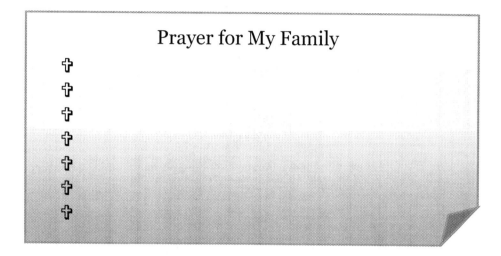

Prayer for My Family

✝
✝
✝
✝
✝
✝
✝

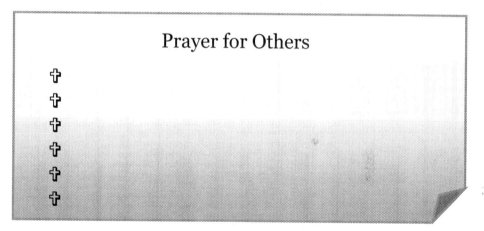

Prayer for Others

✝
✝
✝
✝
✝
✝

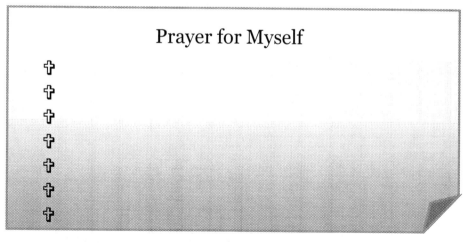

Prayer for Myself

✝
✝
✝
✝
✝
✝
✝

REFLECTION

_____

_____

_____

_____

_____

_____

_____

_____

_____

_____

_____

_____

_____

_____

"You are my war club, my weapon for battle — with you I shatter nations, with you I destroy kingdoms." Jeremiah 51:20 (NIV)

_____

_____

_____

_____

_____

_____

_____

_____

_____

_____

_____

_____

_____

_____

"pray without ceasing"
1 Thessalonians 5:17 (KJV)

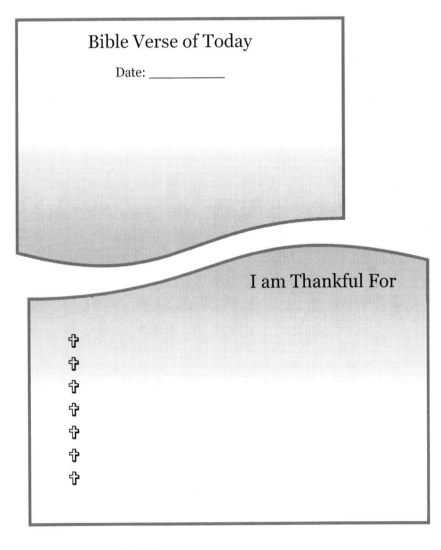

Bible Verse of Today

Date: _____

I am Thankful For

✝
✝
✝
✝
✝
✝
✝

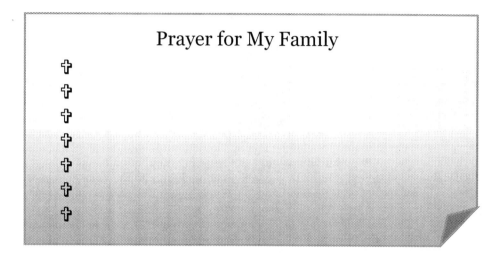

Prayer for My Family

✝
✝
✝
✝
✝
✝
✝

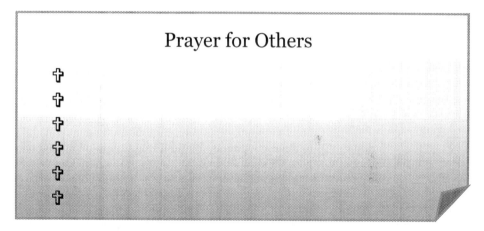

Prayer for Others

✝
✝
✝
✝
✝
✝

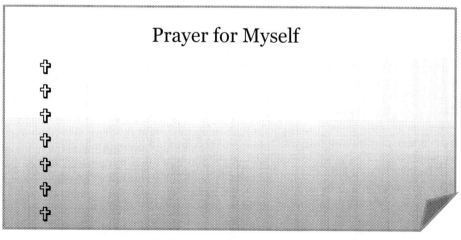

Prayer for Myself

✝
✝
✝
✝
✝
✝
✝

REFLECTION

_____

_____

_____

_____

_____

_____

_____

_____

_____

_____

_____

_____

_____

Use the letters below to describe
yourself or your victory

F
_____

A
_____

V
_____

O
_____

R
_____

Jesus,

I ask that you retrain my thoughts to prioritize chasing things in heaven. In the name of Jesus, I renounce my submission to sin.

The Bible states that the tongue speaks from the richness of the heart. Lord, I ask that you use all of your might to diligently direct my heart. In the name of Jesus, enlarge my mind to think about things that are in heaven.

God, the Bible has helped me to realize that Christ set me free for my freedom and that I should continue to stand and never again be a slave to sin. In the name of Jesus, I ask the Lord to help me resist every wicked temptation through your kindness.

Jeremiah 30:17 (NIV) – But I will restore you to health and heal your wounds,' declares the Lord, 'because you are called an outcast, Zion for whom no one cares.'

We require spiritual assistance in our struggle against Satan, the culture he created, and our inherent shortcomings. God gives us his powerful armor so we might be protected and prevail! Praying should be your lifestyle. Your prayer life is you sacrificing and submitting to God. The sacrifice of praise and adoration for God. Sacrifices are done through fasting and prayer. Regardless of how it may appear when you put on your armor—your must—belief in Jesus. We must pray persistently, hoping and praying following God's will for ourselves, family, and others.

Memorizing verses to memory and reflecting on what the Bible says about you. When facing fear. You should focus on scriptures empowering you to conquer and know God's love. The most excellent way to assist someone in acquiring the entire armor is to pray with them and encourage them to study the Bible. This will enable them to get the sword. Helping someone gain the Helmet through Jesus is equivalent to guiding them toward salvation. Since the armor is only one thing to achieve and one thing to retain, as servants of God, we should assist everyone in getting it. A Christian should educate and prepare the upcoming generation to wear their armor of God every day.

A servant of God should teach and equip the next generation of soldiers in the kingdom of God. Teaching them the word of God and how to live a righteous life. Warrior, be dressed for battle by the Holy Spirit, and all the pieces of your armor will be indestructible by the fiery darts. Your armor is all parts of the puzzle that leads you to wholeness.

Beautiful friend: Always walks in love:1 John 4:18 Even though pure love casts out fear; there is no fear in love.

"But my God shall supply all your need according to his riches in glory by Christ Jesus." Philippians 4:19 (KJV)

ELIZABETH R. WILLIAMS

"pray without ceasing"
1 Thessalonians 5:17 (KJV)

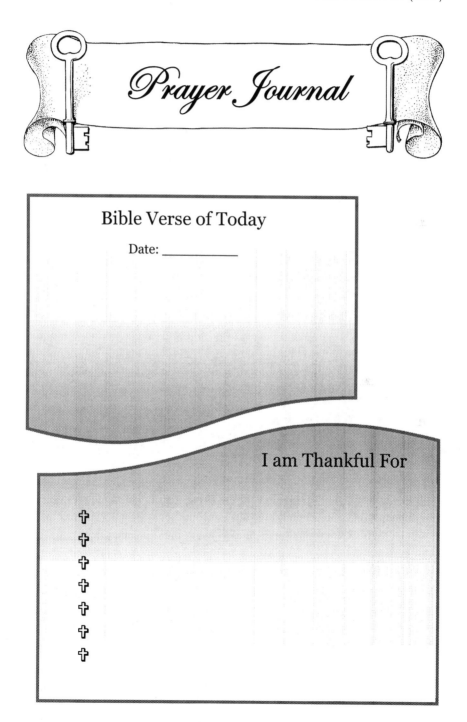

Prayer Journal

Bible Verse of Today

Date: _____

I am Thankful For

✝

✝

✝

✝

✝

✝

✝

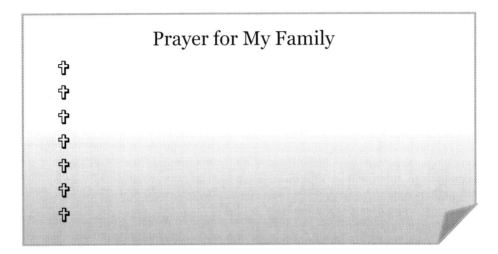

Prayer for My Family

✝
✝
✝
✝
✝
✝
✝

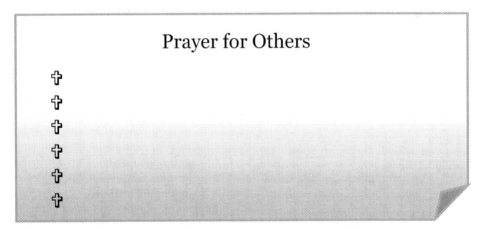

Prayer for Others

✝
✝
✝
✝
✝
✝

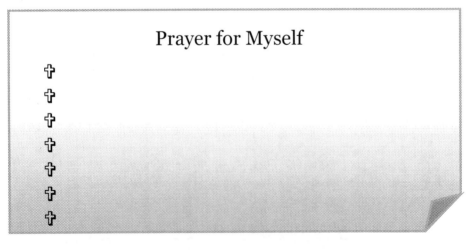

Prayer for Myself

✝
✝
✝
✝
✝
✝
✝

　ELIZABETH R. WILLIAMS

REFLECTION

_____

_____

_____

_____

_____

_____

_____

_____

_____

_____

_____

_____

_____

Use the letters below to describe
yourself or your victory

G

R

A

C

E

"Give, and it shall be given unto you; good measure, pressed down, and shaken together, and running over, shall men give into your bosom. For with the same measure that ye mete withal it shall be measured to you again." Luke 6:38 (KJV)

_____

_____

_____

_____

_____

_____

_____

_____

_____

_____

_____

_____

_____

"pray without ceasing"
1 Thessalonians 5:17 (KJV)

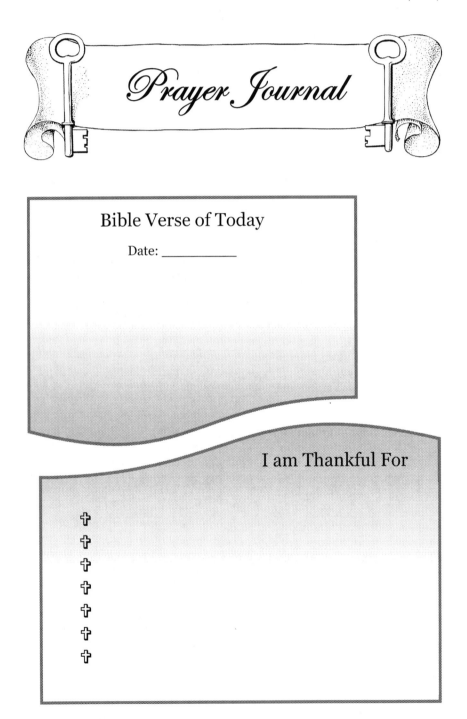

Prayer Journal

Bible Verse of Today

Date: _____

I am Thankful For

✝
✝
✝
✝
✝
✝
✝

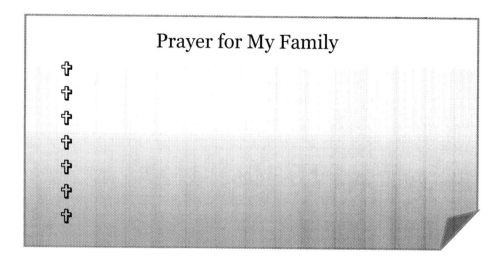

Prayer for My Family

✝
✝
✝
✝
✝
✝
✝

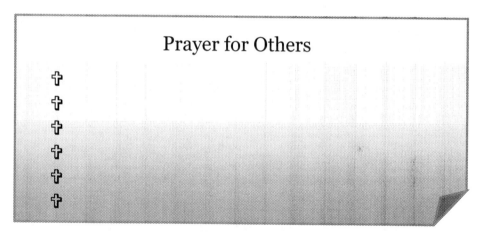

Prayer for Others

✝
✝
✝
✝
✝
✝

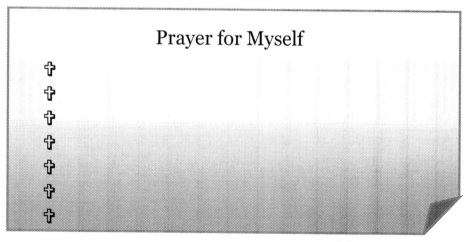

Prayer for Myself

✝
✝
✝
✝
✝
✝
✝

REFLECTION

_____

_____

_____

_____

_____

_____

_____

_____

_____

_____

_____

_____

_____

_____

ELIZABETH R. WILLIAMS

"Every good gift and every perfect gift is from above, and cometh down from the Father of lights, with whom is no variableness, neither shadow of turning." James 1:17 (KJV)

Prayer Journal

Bible Verse of Today

Date: _____

I am Thankful For

✝
✝
✝
✝
✝
✝
✝

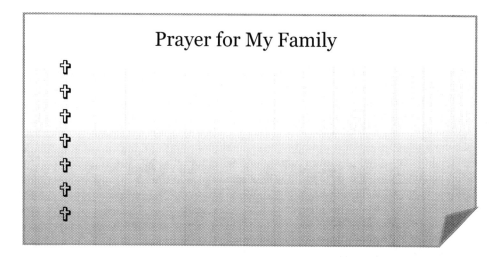

Prayer for My Family

☩
☩
☩
☩
☩
☩
☩

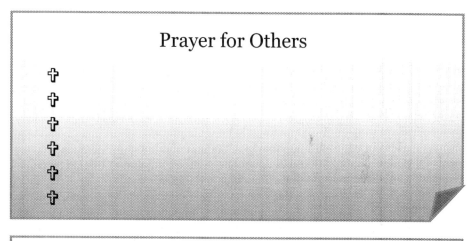

Prayer for Others

☩
☩
☩
☩
☩
☩

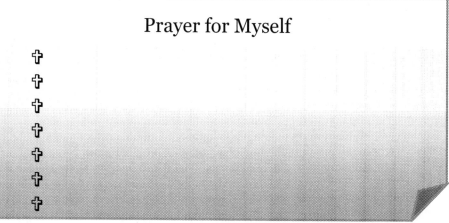

Prayer for Myself

☩
☩
☩
☩
☩
☩
☩

REFLECTION

_____

_____

_____

_____

_____

_____

_____

_____

_____

_____

_____

_____

_____

Use the letters below to describe yourself or your victory

G
_____

U
_____

A
_____

R
_____

D
_____

"Fear thou not; for I am with thee: be not dismayed; for I am thy God: I will strengthen thee; yea, I will help thee; yea, I will uphold thee with the right hand of my righteousness." Isaiah 41:10 (KJV)

_____

_____

_____

_____

_____

_____

_____

_____

_____

_____

_____

_____

ELIZABETH R. WILLIAMS

"pray without ceasing"
1 Thessalonians 5:17 (KJV)

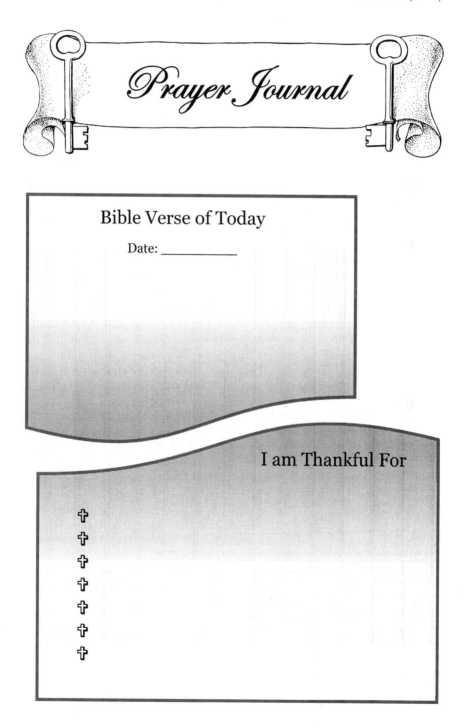

Prayer Journal

Bible Verse of Today

Date: _____

I am Thankful For

✝
✝
✝
✝
✝
✝
✝

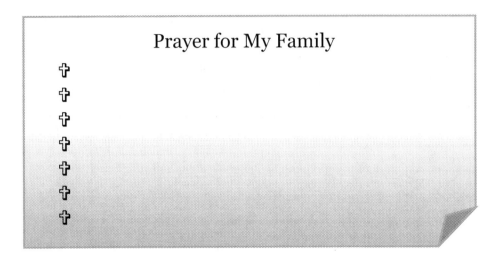

Prayer for My Family

✝
✝
✝
✝
✝
✝
✝

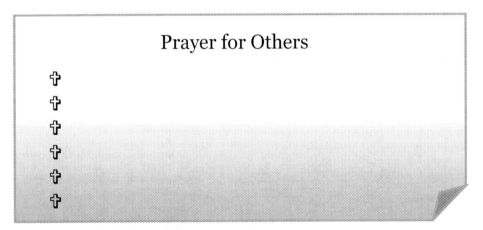

Prayer for Others

✝
✝
✝
✝
✝
✝

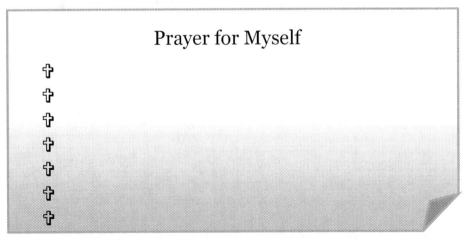

Prayer for Myself

✝
✝
✝
✝
✝
✝
✝

ELIZABETH R. WILLIAMS

REFLECTION

_____

_____

_____

_____

_____

_____

_____

_____

_____

_____

_____

_____

_____

"Instead of your shame you shall have double honor, And instead of confusion they shall rejoice in their portion.

Therefore, in their land they shall possess double; Everlasting joy shall be theirs." Isaiah 61:7 (NKJV)

ELIZABETH R. WILLIAMS

"pray without ceasing"
1 Thessalonians 5:17 (KJV)

Prayer Journal

Bible Verse of Today

Date: _____

I am Thankful For

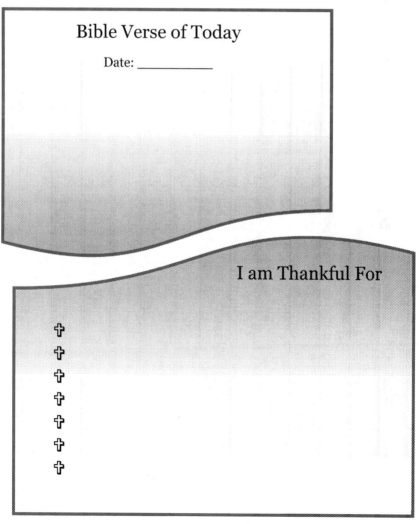

✝

✝

✝

✝

✝

✝

✝

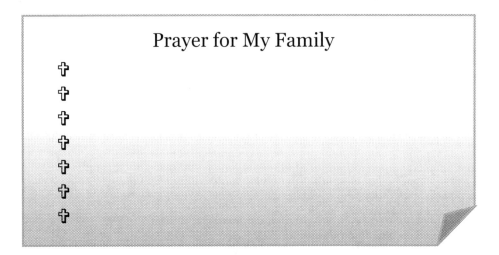

Prayer for My Family

✝
✝
✝
✝
✝
✝
✝

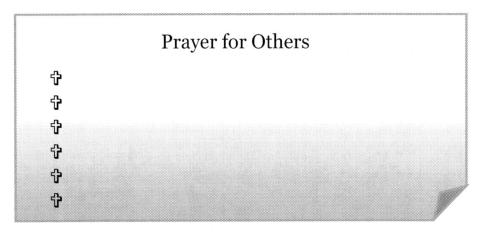

Prayer for Others

✝
✝
✝
✝
✝
✝

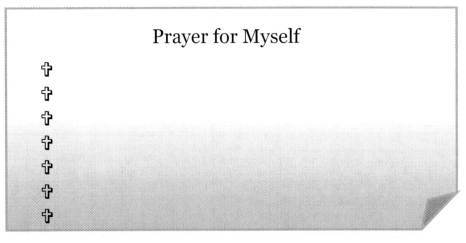

Prayer for Myself

✝
✝
✝
✝
✝
✝
✝

REFLECTION

_____

_____

_____

_____

_____

_____

_____

_____

_____

_____

_____

_____

_____

Take ye heed, watch and pray: for ye know not when the time is. Mark 13:33 (KJV)

ELIZABETH R. WILLIAMS

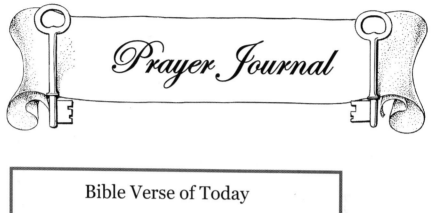

Bible Verse of Today

Date: _____

I am Thankful For

✝

✝

✝

✝

✝

✝

✝

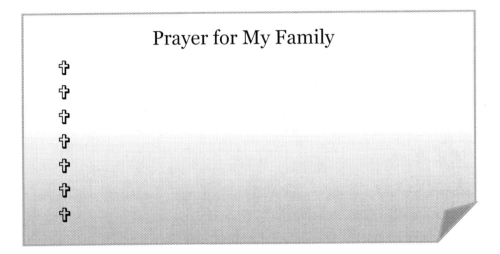

Prayer for My Family

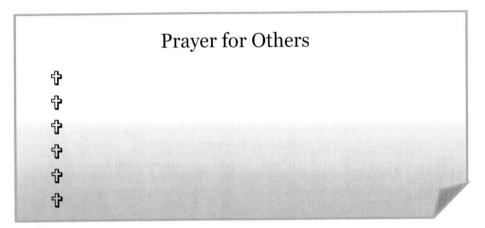

Prayer for Others

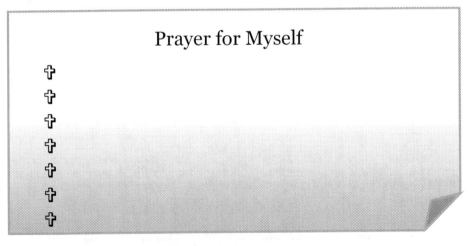

Prayer for Myself

ELIZABETH R. WILLIAMS

REFLECTION

_____

_____

_____

_____

_____

_____

_____

_____

_____

_____

_____

_____

_____

Use the letters below to describe
yourself or your victory

D _____

E _____

L _____

I _____

V _____

E _____

R _____

A _____

N _____

C _____

E _____

It is well with my soul. Psalm 62:5 (NIV)

Prayer Journal

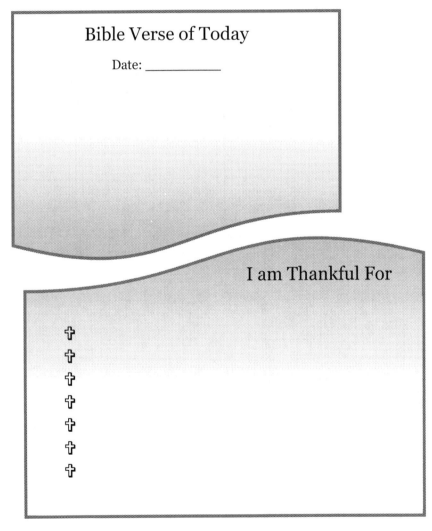

Bible Verse of Today

Date: _____

I am Thankful For

ELIZABETH R. WILLIAMS

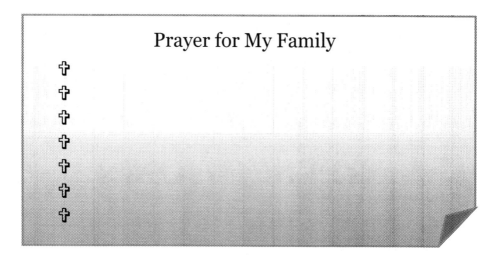

Prayer for My Family

✝
✝
✝
✝
✝
✝
✝

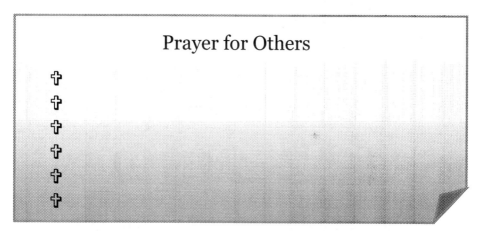

Prayer for Others

✝
✝
✝
✝
✝
✝

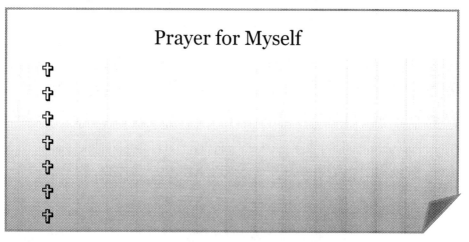

Prayer for Myself

✝
✝
✝
✝
✝
✝
✝

REFLECTION

So, humble yourself under the mighty power of God, and at the right time he will lift you up in honor." 1Peter 5:6 (NLT)

"pray without ceasing"
1 Thessalonians 5:17 (KJV)

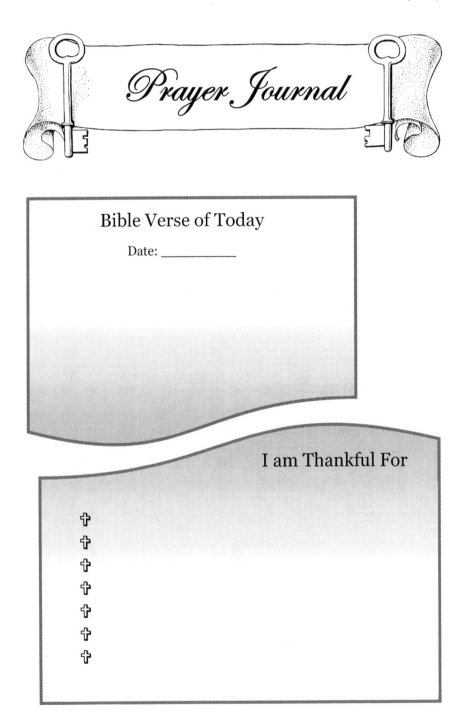

Prayer Journal

Bible Verse of Today

Date: _____

I am Thankful For

✝
✝
✝
✝
✝
✝
✝

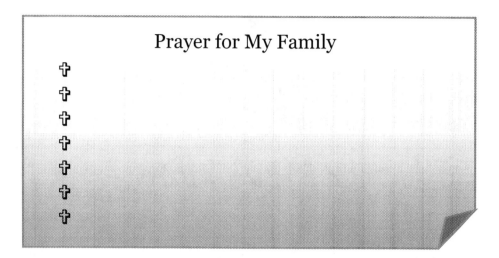

Prayer for My Family

✝
✝
✝
✝
✝
✝
✝

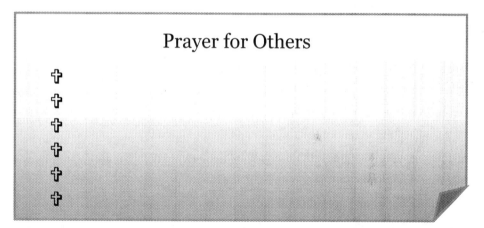

Prayer for Others

✝
✝
✝
✝
✝
✝

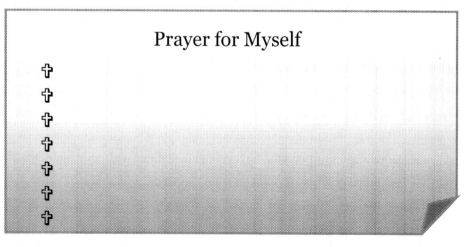

Prayer for Myself

✝
✝
✝
✝
✝
✝
✝

REFLECTION

_____

_____

_____

_____

_____

_____

_____

_____

_____

_____

_____

_____

Use the letters below to describe yourself or your victory

A

R

M

Y

Remember, therefore what you have received and heard; hold it fast, and repent. But if you do not wake up, I will come like a thief, and you will not know at what time I will come to you."
Revelation 3:3 (NIV)

ELIZABETH R. WILLIAMS

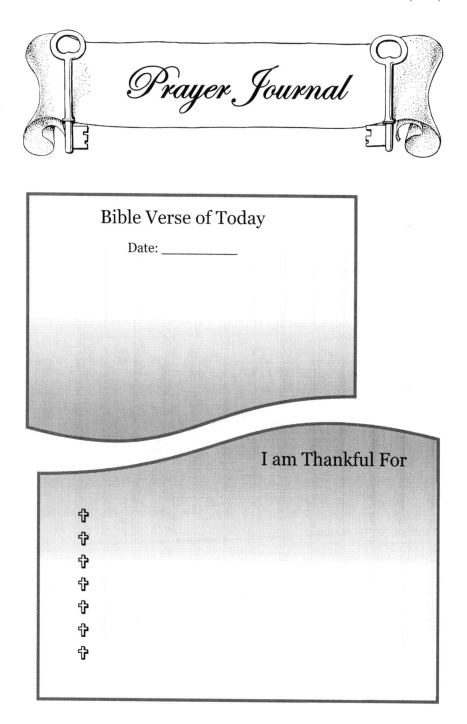

Prayer Journal

Bible Verse of Today

Date: _____

I am Thankful For

✝
✝
✝
✝
✝
✝
✝

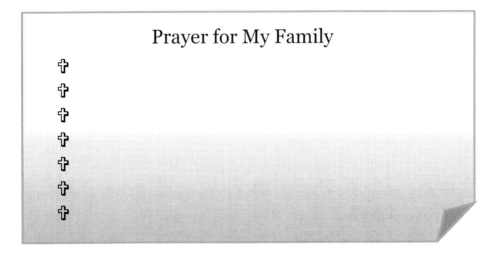

Prayer for My Family

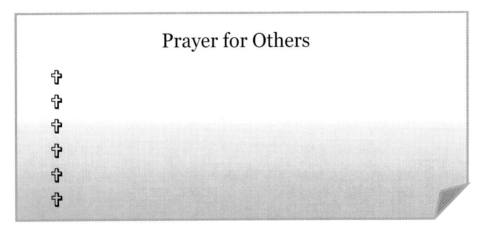

Prayer for Others

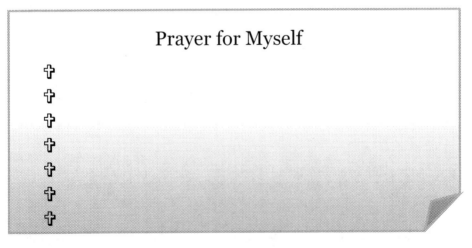

Prayer for Myself

ELIZABETH R. WILLIAMS

REFLECTION

_____

_____

_____

_____

_____

_____

_____

_____

_____

_____

_____

_____

_____

_____

For the LORD protects the bones of the righteous; not one of them is broken. Psalm 34:20 (NIV)

ELIZABETH R. WILLIAMS

"pray without ceasing"
1 Thessalonians 5:17 (KJV)

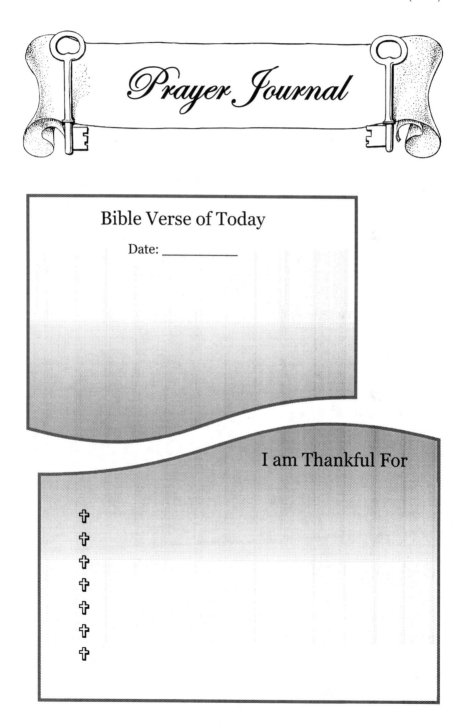

Prayer Journal

Bible Verse of Today

Date: _____

I am Thankful For

✝
✝
✝
✝
✝
✝
✝

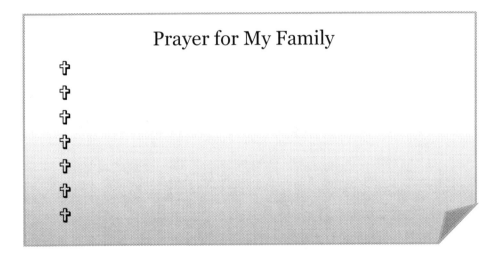

Prayer for My Family

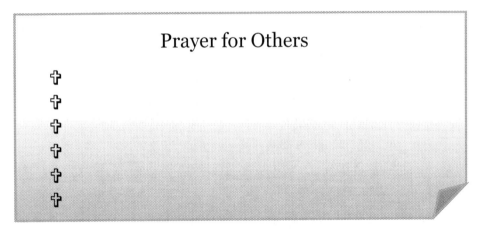

Prayer for Others

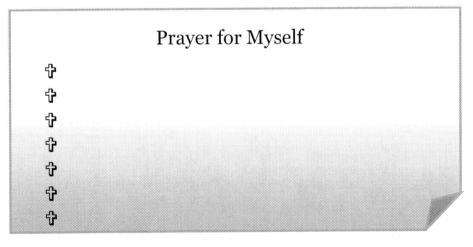

Prayer for Myself

ELIZABETH R. WILLIAMS

REFLECTION

_____

_____

_____

_____

_____

_____

_____

_____

_____

_____

_____

_____

_____

You are my hiding place; You preserve me from trouble; You surround me with songs of deliverance. Selah. Psalm 32:7 (NIV)

ELIZABETH R. WILLIAMS

"pray without ceasing"
1 Thessalonians 5:17 (KJV)

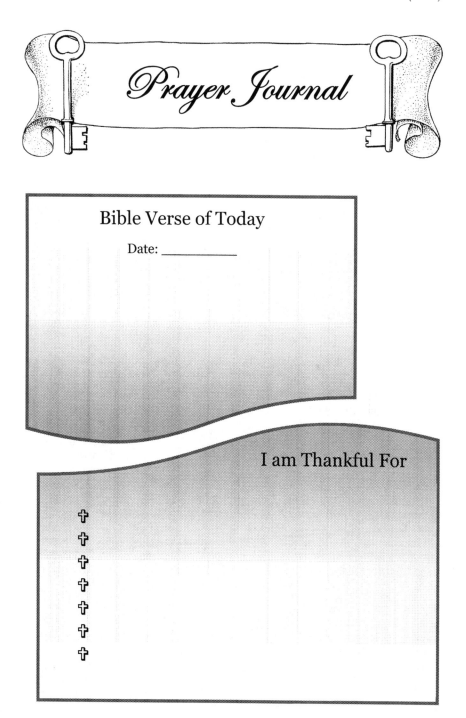

Prayer Journal

Bible Verse of Today

Date: _____

I am Thankful For

✝
✝
✝
✝
✝
✝
✝

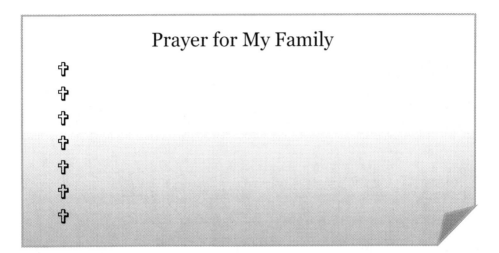

Prayer for My Family

✝
✝
✝
✝
✝
✝
✝

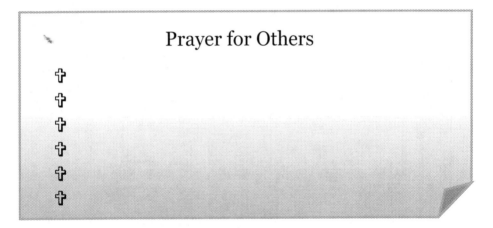

Prayer for Others

✝
✝
✝
✝
✝
✝

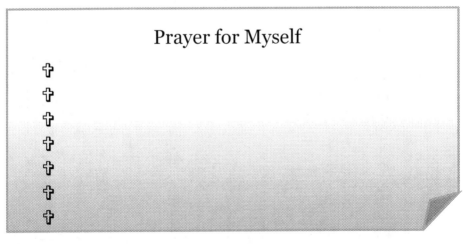

Prayer for Myself

✝
✝
✝
✝
✝
✝
✝

REFLECTION

_____

_____

_____

_____

_____

_____

_____

_____

_____

_____

_____

_____

_____

Use the letters below to describe
yourself or your victory

W _____

O _____

R _____

D _____

O _____

F _____

G _____

O _____

D _____

ELIZABETH R. WILLIAMS

> *Thou therefore endure hardness, as a good soldier of Jesus Christ."* 2 Timothy 2:3 (KJV)

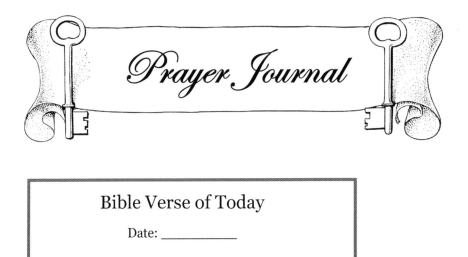

Bible Verse of Today

Date: _____

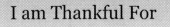

I am Thankful For

✝
✝
✝
✝
✝
✝
✝

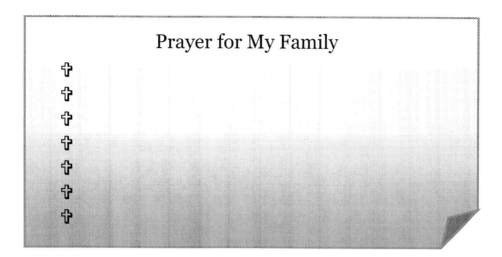

Prayer for My Family

✝
✝
✝
✝
✝
✝
✝

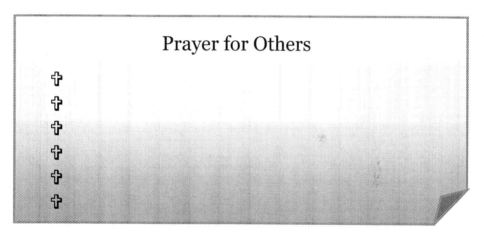

Prayer for Others

✝
✝
✝
✝
✝
✝

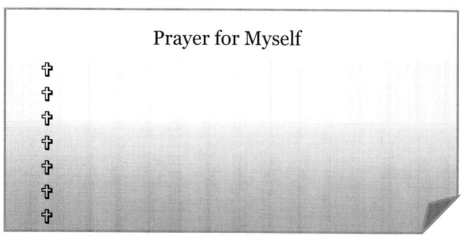

Prayer for Myself

✝
✝
✝
✝
✝
✝
✝

REFLECTION

_____

_____

_____

_____

_____

_____

_____

_____

_____

_____

_____

_____

For we do not wrestle against flesh and blood, but against the rulers, against the authorities, against the cosmic powers over this present darkness, against the spiritual forces of evil in the heavenly places. Ephesians 6:12 (ESV)

_____

_____

_____

_____

_____

_____

_____

_____

_____

_____

_____

_____

Prayer Journal

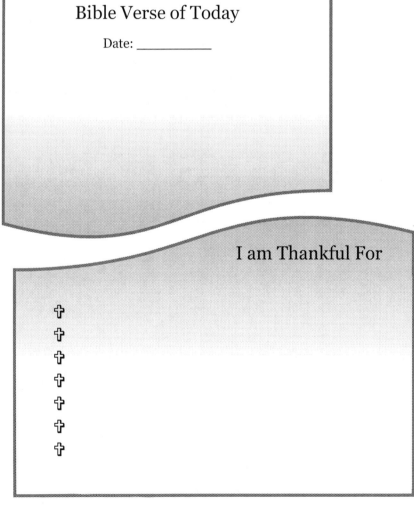

Bible Verse of Today

Date: _____

I am Thankful For

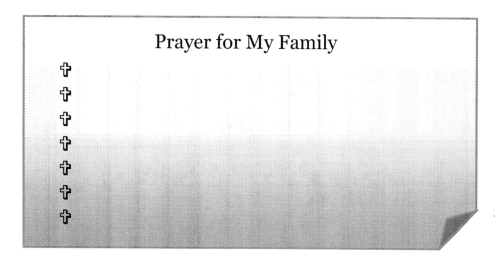

Prayer for My Family

✝
✝
✝
✝
✝
✝
✝

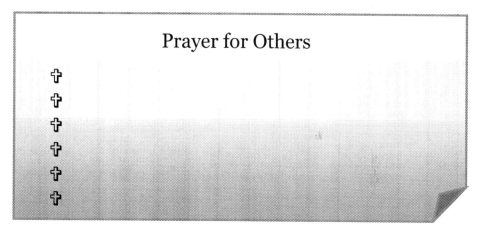

Prayer for Others

✝
✝
✝
✝
✝
✝

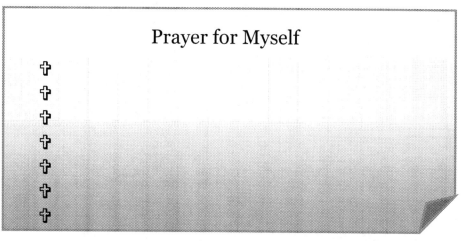

Prayer for Myself

✝
✝
✝
✝
✝
✝
✝

REFLECTION

ELIZABETH R. WILLIAMS

I pray that out of his glorious riches he may strengthen you with power through his Spirit in your inner being, so that Christ may dwell in your hearts through faith. And I pray that you, being rooted and established in love. Ephesians 3:16-17 (NIV)

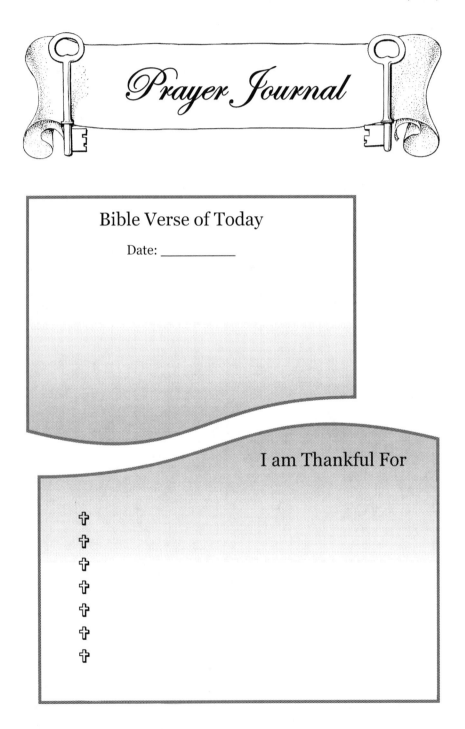

Prayer Journal

Bible Verse of Today

Date: _____

I am Thankful For

✝
✝
✝
✝
✝
✝
✝

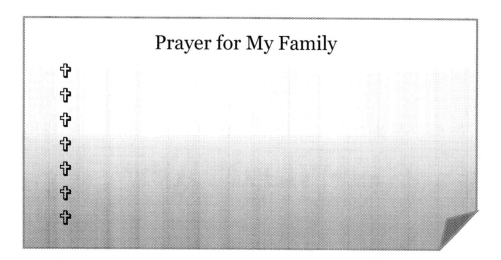

Prayer for My Family

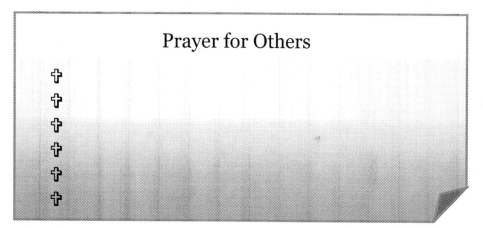

Prayer for Others

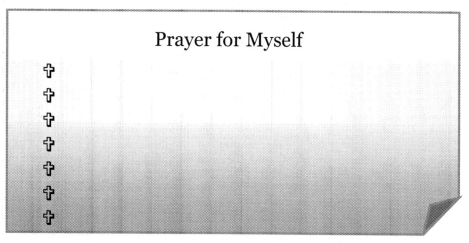

Prayer for Myself

REFLECTION

_____

_____

_____

_____

_____

_____

_____

_____

_____

_____

_____

_____

_____

_____

Use the letters below to describe yourself or your victory

H _____

E _____

A _____

L _____

I _____

N _____

G _____

For I am the LORD, your God, who takes hold of your right hand and says to you, Do not fear; I will help you. Isaiah 41:13 (NIV)

ELIZABETH R. WILLIAMS

"pray without ceasing"
1 Thessalonians 5:17 (KJV)

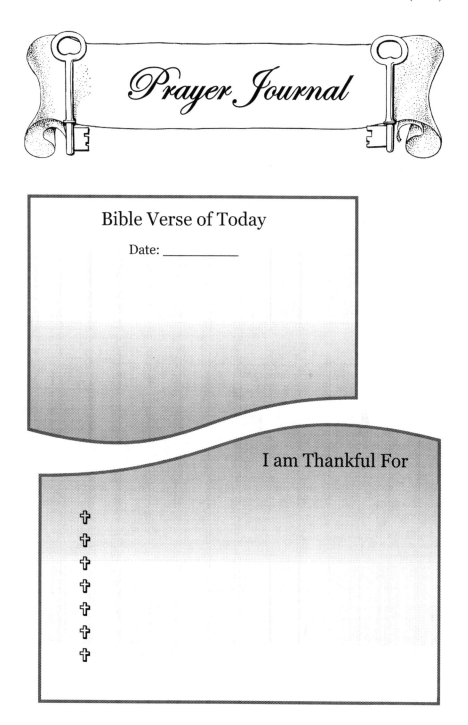

Prayer Journal

Bible Verse of Today

Date: _____

I am Thankful For

✝
✝
✝
✝
✝
✝
✝

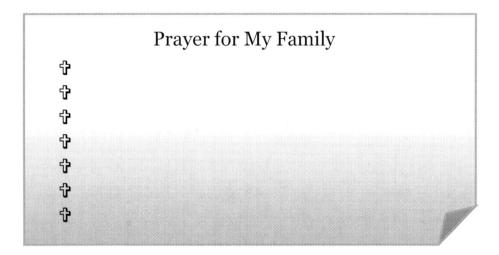

Prayer for My Family

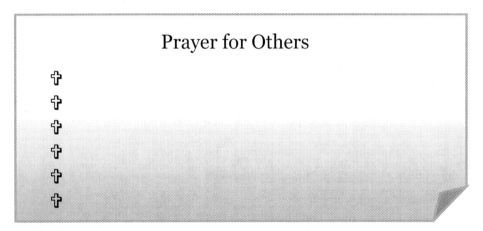

Prayer for Others

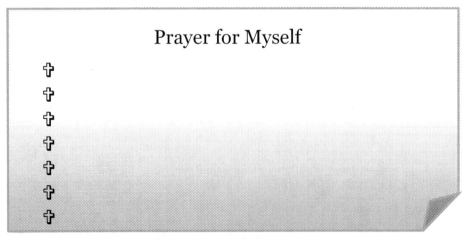

Prayer for Myself

ELIZABETH R. WILLIAMS

REFLECTION

_____

_____

_____

_____

_____

_____

_____

_____

_____

_____

_____

_____

_____

_____

For the word of God is alive and active. Sharper than any double-edged sword, it penetrates even to dividing soul and spirit, joints and marrow; it judges the thoughts and attitudes of the heart. Hebrews 4:12 (NIV)

"pray without ceasing"
1 Thessalonians 5:17 (KJV)

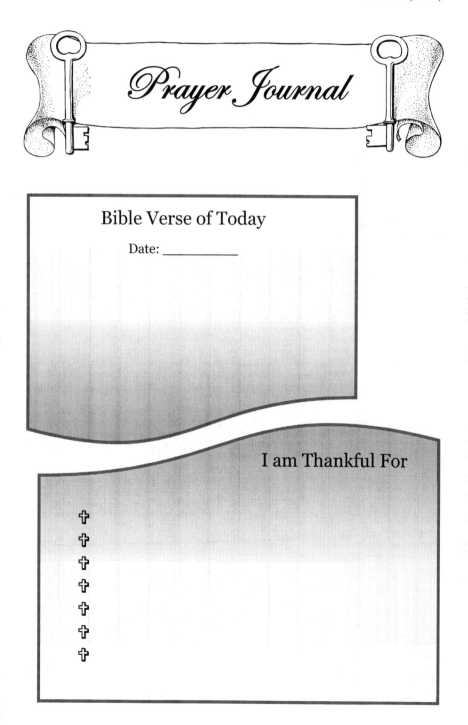

Prayer Journal

Bible Verse of Today

Date: _____

I am Thankful For

✝
✝
✝
✝
✝
✝
✝

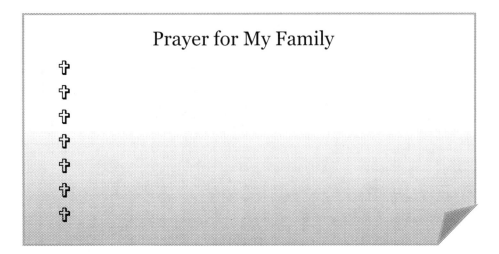

Prayer for My Family

☦
☦
☦
☦
☦
☦
☦

Prayer for Others

☦
☦
☦
☦
☦
☦

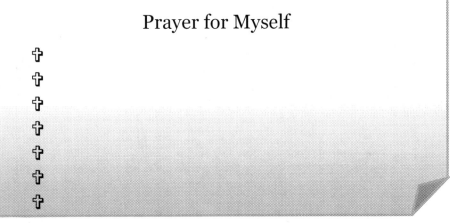

Prayer for Myself

☦
☦
☦
☦
☦
☦
☦

REFLECTION

_____

_____

_____

_____

_____

_____

_____

_____

_____

_____

_____

_____

_____

_____

REMAIN WEARING YOUR ARMOR EVERY DAY.

Wearing your armor should be your way of life; don't just put it on when you are about to pray. Psalm 37:7 urges us to surrender our lives to God. From all your misdeeds, repent. Request a new infusion of the Holy Spirit. Break agreements and curses that give them authority over your life. Pray more fervently. Give up any connections with strongmen and strongholds, occult sea spirits, familiar spirits, and spirits of the air, water, and soil. Continuously rely on the Holy Spirit for strength. Accept and reaffirm that Jesus Christ has given you freedom. Say and accept what the Lord says about you.

BEAUTIFUL WARRIOR:
REPEAT THIS PRAYER

Every occult force trying to damage my life is paralyzed in the name of Jesus Christ. I order every stubborn power engaged with removing me from my position of dominance to weaken and be eliminated in the name of Jesus. I disavow any agreement that tie me to unfavorable relationships in the name of Jesus. I repudiate any contract that binds my body, soul, and spirit to the occult in the name of Jesus. All soul ties in my bloodline are rendered impotent in the name of Jesus. In the name of Jesus, I renounce any negative influence on my life.

I refuel my body, soul, and spirit with Jesus' blood. I declare that I have been wholly freed through the blood of Jesus. In the name of Jesus, I cut off every branch that is not bearing fruit in my academic pursuits, psychological wellness, finances, spiritual growth, marriage, children, and partnerships.

I AM MORE THAN A CONQUEROR.
I AM JOYFUL, KIND, LOVING, STRONG AND BEAUTIFUL.
I AM NOT WHO I WAS! I FORGIVE MYSELF.
I AM ACCEPTABLE. I AM FORGIVEN.

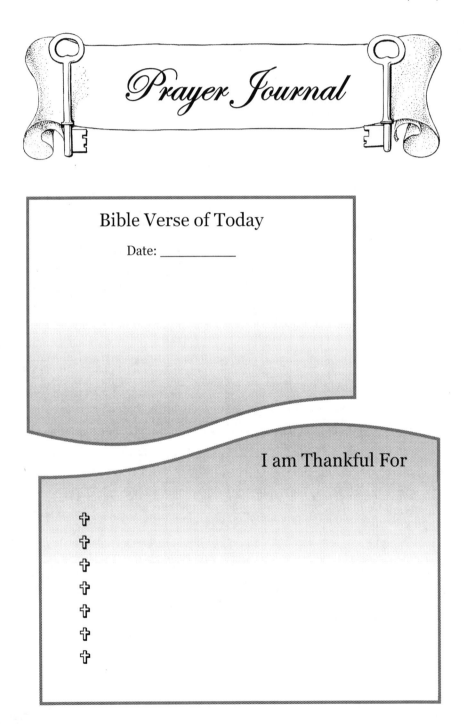

Prayer Journal

Bible Verse of Today

Date: _____

I am Thankful For

✟
✟
✟
✟
✟
✟
✟

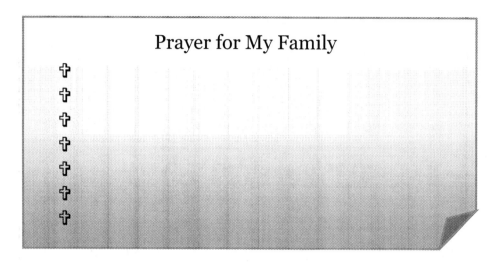

Prayer for My Family

✝
✝
✝
✝
✝
✝
✝

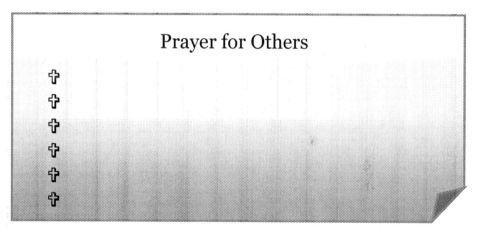

Prayer for Others

✝
✝
✝
✝
✝
✝

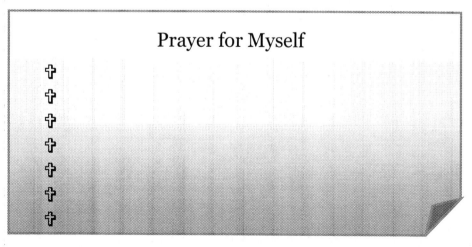

Prayer for Myself

✝
✝
✝
✝
✝
✝
✝

REFLECTION

_____

_____

_____

_____

_____

_____

_____

_____

_____

_____

_____

_____

_____

_____

_____

ELIZABETH R. WILLIAMS

Scripture Writing Plan
Armor of God Scriptures

✍ Psalm 27:1-2, (KJV)
"The Lord is my light and my salvation; whom shall I fear? The Lord is the strength of my life; of whom shall I be afraid? When the wicked, even mine enemies and my foes, came upon me to eat up my flesh, they stumbled and fell."

✍ Hebrews 4:12 (NIV)
For the word of God is living and active. Sharper than any double-edged sword, it penetrates even to dividing soul and spirit, joints, and marrow; it judges the thoughts and attitudes of the heart.

✍ 1Peter 5:8 (NIV)
Be self-controlled and alert. Your enemy, the devil, prowls around like a roaring lion looking for someone to devour.

✍ 1Thessalonians 5:8 (NIV)
But since we belong to the day, let us be self-controlled, putting on faith and love as a breastplate, and the hope of salvation as a helmet.

✍ Romans 13:12-14 (NIV)
12 The night is nearly over; the day is almost here. So let us put aside the deeds of darkness and put on the armor of light. 13 Let us behave decently, as in the daytime, not

in orgies and drunkenness, not in sexual immorality and debauchery, not in dissension and jealousy. 14 Rather, clothe yourselves with the Lord Jesus Christ, and do not think about how to gratify the desires of the sinful nature.

✍ John 14:6 (NIV)
Jesus answered, "I am the way and the truth and the life. No one comes to the Father except through me.

✍ Isaiah 54:16-17 (NIV)
16 "See, it is I who created the blacksmith who fans the coals into flame and forges a weapon fit for its work. And it is I who have created the destroyer to work havoc; 17 no weapon forged against you will prevail, and you will refute every tongue that accuses you. This is the heritage of the servants of the LORD, and this is their vindication from me," declares the LORD.

✍ Romans 10:17 (NIV)
Consequently, faith comes from hearing the message, and the message is heard through the word of Christ.

✍ James 4:7 (NIV)
Submit yourselves, then, to God. Resist the devil, and he will flee from you.

✍ 2 Corinthians 5:21(NIV)
God made him who had no sin to be sin for us, so that in him we might become the righteousness of God.

✍ Romans 16:20 (NIV)
The God of peace will soon crush Satan under your feet. The grace of our Lord Jesus be with you.

ELIZABETH R. WILLIAMS

✍ Isaiah 59:17 (NIV)

He put on righteousness as his breastplate, and the helmet of salvation on his head; he put on the garments of vengeance and wrapped himself in zeal as in a cloak.

✍ 1 Peter 3:15 (NIV)

But in your hearts set apart Christ as Lord. Always be prepared to give an answer to everyone who asks you to give the reason for the hope that you have. But do this with gentleness and respect.

✍ John 3:16 (NIV)

"For God so loved the world that he gave his one and only Son, that whoever believes in him shall not perish but have eternal life.

REFLECTION

_____

_____

_____

_____

_____

_____

_____

_____

_____

_____

_____

_____

_____

ELIZABETH R. WILLIAMS

REFLECTION

_____

_____

_____

_____

_____

_____

_____

_____

_____

_____

_____

_____

_____

REFLECTION

_____

_____

_____

_____

_____

_____

_____

_____

_____

_____

_____

_____

_____

ELIZABETH R. WILLIAMS

REFLECTION

_____

_____

_____

_____

_____

_____

_____

_____

_____

_____

_____

_____

_____

_____

ANSWER KEY

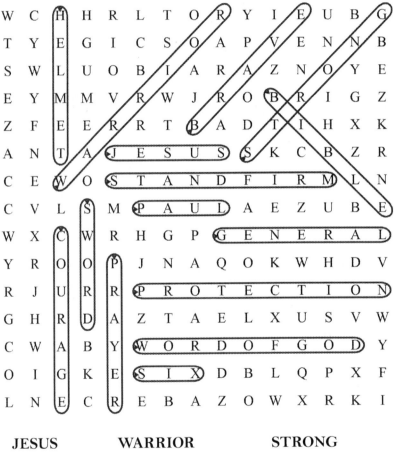

W	C	H	H	R	L	T	O	R	Y	I	E	U	B	G
T	Y	E	G	I	C	S	O	A	P	V	E	N	N	B
S	W	L	U	O	B	I	A	R	A	Z	N	O	Y	E
E	Y	M	M	V	R	W	J	R	O	B	R	I	G	Z
Z	F	E	E	R	R	T	B	A	D	T	I	H	X	K
A	N	T	A	J	E	S	U	S	S	K	C	B	Z	R
C	E	W	O	S	T	A	N	D	F	I	R	M	L	N
C	V	L	S	M	P	A	U	L	A	E	Z	U	B	E
W	X	C	W	R	H	G	P	G	E	N	E	R	A	L
Y	R	O	O	P	J	N	A	Q	O	K	W	H	D	V
R	J	U	R	R	P	R	O	T	E	C	T	I	O	N
G	H	R	D	A	Z	T	A	E	L	X	U	S	V	W
C	W	A	B	Y	W	O	R	D	O	F	G	O	D	Y
O	I	G	K	E	S	I	X	D	B	L	Q	P	X	F
L	N	E	C	R	E	B	A	Z	O	W	X	R	K	I

JESUS	WARRIOR	STRONG
SIX	PRAYER	PROTECTION
BIBLE	HELMET	STAND FIRM
SWORD	GENERAL	BRAVE
PAUL	WORD OF GOD	COURAGE

ANSWER KEY

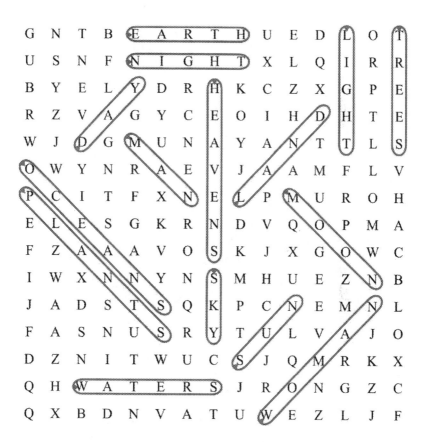

```
G   N   T   B   E   A   R   T   H   U   E   D   L   O   T
U   S   N   F   N   I   G   H   T   X   L   Q   I   R   R
B   Y   E   L   Y   D   R   H   K   C   Z   X   G   P   E
R   Z   V   A   G   Y   C   E   O   I   H   D   H   T   E
W   J   D   G   M   U   N   A   Y   A   N   T   L   S
O   W   Y   N   R   A   E   V   J   A   A   M   F   L   V
P   C   I   T   F   X   N   E   L   P   M   U   R   O   H
E   L   E   S   G   K   R   N   D   V   Q   O   P   M   A
F   Z   A   A   A   V   O   S   K   J   X   G   O   W   C
I   W   X   N   N   Y   N   S   M   H   U   E   Z   N   B
J   A   D   S   T   S   Q   K   P   C   N   E   M   N   L
F   A   S   N   U   S   R   Y   T   U   L   V   A   J   O
D   Z   N   I   T   W   U   C   S   J   Q   M   R   K   X
Q   H   W   A   T   E   R   S   J   R   O   N   G   Z   C
Q   X   B   D   N   V   A   T   U   W   E   Z   L   J   F
```

HEAVENS	MAN	PLANTS
SKY	WATERS	TREES
MOON	OCEANS	DAY
EARTH	WOMAN	SUN
LAND	LIGHT	

ANSWER KEY

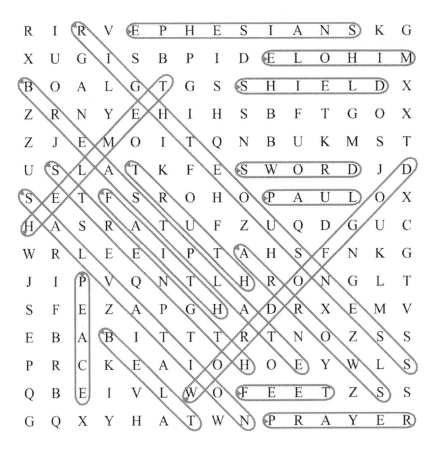

R	I	R	V	E	P	H	E	S	I	A	N	S	K	G
X	U	G	I	S	B	P	I	D	E	L	O	H	I	M
B	O	A	L	G	T	G	S	S	H	I	E	L	D	X
Z	R	N	Y	E	H	I	H	S	B	F	T	G	O	X
Z	J	E	M	O	I	T	Q	N	B	U	K	M	S	T
U	S	L	A	T	K	F	E	S	W	O	R	D	J	D
S	E	T	F	S	R	O	H	O	P	A	U	L	O	X
H	A	S	R	A	T	U	F	Z	U	Q	D	G	U	C
W	R	L	E	E	I	P	T	A	H	S	F	N	K	G
J	I	P	V	Q	N	T	L	H	R	O	N	G	L	T
S	F	E	Z	A	P	G	H	A	D	R	X	E	M	V
E	B	A	B	I	T	T	T	R	T	N	O	Z	S	S
P	R	C	K	E	A	I	O	H	O	E	Y	W	L	S
Q	B	E	I	V	L	W	O	F	E	E	T	Z	S	S
G	Q	X	Y	H	A	T	W	N	P	R	A	Y	E	R

FAITH	SWORD	ELOHIM
FEET	PAUL	STRENGTH
EPHESIANS	PRAYER	BREASTPLATE
RIGHTEOUSNESS	SALVATION	SHIELD
ARROWS	HELMET	BELT
TRUTH	PEACE	

ANSWER KEY

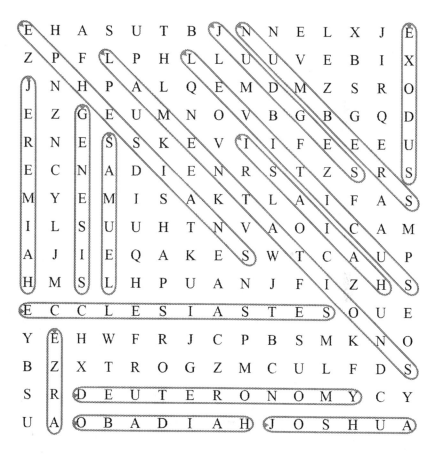

E	H	A	S	U	T	B	J	N	N	E	L	X	J	E
Z	P	F	L	P	H	L	L	U	U	V	E	B	I	X
J	N	H	P	A	L	Q	E	M	D	M	Z	S	R	O
E	Z	G	E	U	M	N	O	V	B	G	B	G	Q	D
R	N	E	S	S	K	E	V	I	I	F	E	E	E	U
E	C	N	A	D	I	E	N	R	S	T	Z	S	R	S
M	Y	E	M	I	S	A	K	T	L	A	I	F	A	S
I	L	S	U	U	H	T	N	V	A	O	I	C	A	M
A	J	I	E	Q	A	K	E	S	W	T	C	A	U	P
H	M	S	L	H	P	U	A	N	J	F	I	Z	H	S
E	C	C	L	E	S	I	A	S	T	E	S	O	U	E
Y	E	H	W	F	R	J	C	P	B	S	M	K	N	O
B	Z	X	T	R	O	G	Z	M	C	U	L	F	D	S
S	R	D	E	U	T	E	R	O	N	O	M	Y	C	Y
U	A	O	B	A	D	I	A	H	J	O	S	H	U	A

GENESIS	**OBADIAH**	**CHRONICLES**
EXODUS	**LAMENTATIONS**	**EZRA**
LEVITICUS	**ECCLESIASTES**	**ISAIAH**
NUMBERS	**DEUTERONOMY**	**JUDGES**
JOSHUA	**SAMUEL**	**JEREMIAH**

ANSWER KEY

```
O  R  G  K  I  Y  Y  M  U  B  A  Q  S  C  N
Z  F  U  M  O  S  G  T  A  G  A  I  N  S  T
U  Q  A  J  Y  F  E  V  J  T  E  L  D  L  W
P  F  Q  I  L  Z  N  D  A  H  C  O  R  K  J
W  E  V  E  T  N  T  D  F  G  C  N  U  Z  T
M  G  A  U  O  H  L  Q  V  K  Z  G  D  S  M
X  E  I  C  Q  E  E  Y  G  J  C  S  K  N  P
V  N  E  R  E  I  N  O  W  Y  A  U  J  K  M
F  P  R  K  H  L  E  E  T  J  A  F  S  M  Z
U  R  W  E  N  T  S  Q  R  E  C  F  L  B  H
Z  Y  U  U  K  E  S  L  V  H  M  E  X  C  V
X  F  S  I  J  P  S  O  H  N  D  R  K  C  Q
I  P  Q  H  T  K  L  S  B  D  V  I  L  T  J
T  E  M  P  E  R  A  N  C  E  A  N  S  U  V
H  O  L  Y  S  P  I  R  I  T  W  G  L  A  W
```

HOLY SPIRIT	**FAITH**	**TEMPERANCE**
LOVE	**LONG**	**MEEKNESS**
JOY	**SUFFERING**	**FRUIT**
AGAINST	**LAW**	
PEACE		
GENTLENESS		

ELIZABETH R. WILLIAMS

ANSWER KEY

1) e i a p s n h s e   Ephesians

2) y r a p e r   prayer

3) o r a r r i w   warrior

4) s x i   six

5) e s j s u   Jesus

6) a p u l   Paul

7) o c u e g r a   courage

8) d s r e o i l   solider

9) n d i a f m s r t   stand firm

10) r h s n t g e t   strength

11) h e i l o m   Elohim

12) e v a r b   brave

13) o g r o f d o d w   word of God

14) e i b b l   bible

15) l e e g n a r   general

Printed in the United States
by Baker & Taylor Publisher Services